AMERICAN TROUBLEMAKERS

Ida B. Wells: Antilynching Crusader

AMERICAN TROUBLEMAKERS

Titles in Series

Cesar Chavez by Burnham Holmes

Jefferson Davis by Robert R. Potter

Mother Jones by Joan C. Hawxhurst

Thomas Paine by Karin Clafford Farley

Sitting Bull by Steven Bodow

Ida B. Wells by Richard M. Haynes

AMERICAN TROUBLEMAKERS

IDA B. WELLS:
Antilynching Crusader

Richard M. Haynes

With an Introduction by James P. Shenton

RAINTREE
STECK-VAUGHN
PUBLISHERS
The Steck-Vaughn Company

Austin, Texas

To Robert and Ruth Haynes with love and appreciation.

Copyright © 1994 Steck-Vaughn Company

All rights reserved. No part of this book may be reproduced or utilized in any form or by any means, electronic or mechanical, including photocopying, recording, or by any information storage and retrieval system, without permission in writing from the publisher. Inquiries should be addressed to: Steck-Vaughn Company, P.O. Box 26015, Austin, TX 78755.

CONSULTANTS

Elizabeth Blackmar
Associate Professor of History
Department of History
Columbia College
New York, New York

Jessie B. Gladden
Division Specialist
Office of Social Studies
Baltimore City Schools
Baltimore, Maryland

MANAGING EDITOR
Richard G. Gallin

PROJECT MANAGER
Julie Klaus

PHOTO EDITOR
Margie Foster

A Gallin House Press Book

Library of Congress Cataloging-in-Publication Data
Haynes, Richard M.
    Ida B. Wells / written by Richard M. Haynes.
      p.   cm. — (American Troublemakers)
    "A Gallin House Press Book."—T.p. verso.
    Includes bibliographical references and index.
    Summary: Describes the life of the black woman journalist who was born into slavery and conducted a lifelong crusade for the civil rights of various minorities.
    ISBN 0-8114-2325-5
    1. Wells-Barnett, Ida B., 1862-1931 — Juvenile literature.   2. Afro-Americans—Biography—Juvenile literature.   3. Afro-American women—Biography—Juvenile literature.   4. Civil rights workers—United States—Biography—Juvenile literature.   [1. Wells-Barnett. Ida. B., 1862-1931. 2. Civil rights workers. 3. Afro-Americans—Biography.] I.Title. II. Series.
E185.97.W55H38   1994
323'.092—dc20
[B]   92-22192
                                                                                      CIP
                                                                                        AC

Printed and bound in the United States.

1 2 3 4 5 6 7 8 9 0   LB   98 97 96 95 94 93

CONTENTS

Introduction by James P. Shenton 7
1   Born a Slave...9
2   Head of the Family...21
3   Getting Established in Memphis.......................30
4   Finding a Cause 36
5   Beginning the Crusade....................................48
6   On the World Stage 55
7   Torn Between Family and Cause 68
8   Continuing Battles 77
9   Disappointment and Determination..................88
10 Final Gifts 99

Key Dates..113
Glossary..116
Bibliography and Recommended Readings...............119
Places to Visit 120
Index..121

Map
Key Places in Ida B. Well's United States 25

Ida B. Wells (Ida B. Wells-Barnett, after her marriage in 1895)

INTRODUCTION

by James P. Shenton

Biography is the history of the individual lives of men and women. In all lives, there is a sequence that begins with birth, evolves into the development of character in childhood and adolescence, is followed by the emergence of maturity in adulthood, and finally concludes with death. All lives follow this pattern, although with each emerge the differences that make each life unique. These distinctive characteristics are usually determined by the particular area in which a person has been most active. An artist draws his or her specific identity from the area of the arts in which he or she has been most active. So the writer becomes an author; the musician, a performer or composer; the politician, a senator, governor, president, or statesperson. The intellectual discipline to which one is attached identifies the scientist, historian, economist, literary critic, or political scientist, among many. Some aspects of human behavior are identified as heroic, cowardly, corrupt, or just ordinary. The task of the biographer is to explain why a particular life is worth remembering. And if the effort is successful, the reader draws from it insights into a vast range of behavior patterns. In a sense, biography provides lessons from life.

Some lives become important because of the position a person holds. Typical would be that of a U.S. President in which a biographer compares the various incumbents to determine their comparative importance. Without question, Abraham Lincoln was a profoundly significant President, much more so than Warren G. Harding, whose administration was swamped by corruption. Others achieve importance because of their role in a particular area. So Emily Dickinson and Carl Sandburg are recognized as important poets and Albert Einstein as a great scientist.

Implicit in the choice of biographical subjects is the idea that each somehow affected history. Their lives explain something about the world in which they lived, even as they affect our lives and that of generations to come. But there is another consideration: Some lives are more interesting than those of others. Within each life is a great story that illuminates human behavior.

Then there are those people who are troublemakers, people whom we cannot ignore. They are the people who both upset and fascinate us. Their singular quality is that they are uniquely different. Troublemakers are irritating, perhaps frightening, frustrating, and disturbing, but never dull. They march to their own drummer, and they are original.

One of the more painful aspects of American history was the system of racial segregation imposed on African Americans between the 1880s and the mid-1960s. When first created, this system was often enforced through "lynch law." Under lynch law, people accused of breaking laws were not tried by judge and jury but by mobs. Several thousand black men, women, and children were lynched. More often than not, these murders were unbelievably brutal. Hanging, burning at the stake, torture, and beatings to death were typical examples. Aware that most white-controlled Southern state governments were not ready to use their power to punish lynching, Ida B. Wells concluded that a federal law banning the act was necessary.

The remarkable fact is that Ida B. Wells made antilynching her cause. Born a slave in Mississippi and left as an orphan at 16, she took responsibility for raising her brothers and sisters. As a teacher in Tennessee, she forthrightly criticized the inferior education given African-American children. Fired from her teaching position, Wells began to work full-time as the editor and part owner of *Free Speech*, a black newspaper. After three of her friends were lynched in 1892, her vigorous editorials denouncing lynching aroused controversy. A mob wrecked her newspaper office, and she decided to shift her work to New York and Chicago.

Her antilynching articles, books, and lectures gained international attention. When Ida B. Wells met with President William McKinley to push for federal antilynching legislation, her name and the struggle became synonymous. With great vigor, she also fought for women's suffrage, set up African-American community organizations in Chicago, and helped found the NAACP. It took courage to investigate lynchings and report the gruesome facts, but she believed that an America with full justice for all required a willingness to make a total commitment. When Ida B. Wells died in 1931, the fight was far from over, but her example had made her a legend.

Born a Slave

"Jim and Lizzie Wells have both died of the fever. They died within twenty-four hours of each other. The children are all at home . . . and [some caring people have] put a woman there to take care of them. Send word to Ida." Ida B. Wells was only 16 when this letter arrived in the early fall of 1878. It changed her life forever.

Ida had been visiting on her grandmother's farm when the letter arrived. Because she was the oldest of Jim and Lizzie Wells's seven children, Ida knew she had to return home immediately. On her way, Ida must have thought about her mother and father, and the hard times through which they had brought her.

Ida Bell Wells had been born into slavery on July 16, 1862, in Holly Springs, Mississippi. Both of her parents had been born into slavery as well. Her father, James, had been born on the farm Ida was visiting when the letter arrived. It was in neighboring Tippah County, more than 20 miles from the Wells family's home in Holly Springs.

James Wells was the son of Peggy, who had been a slave on the farm, and her white owner. James Wells's master-father had given his last name to his son but had continued to live with his white wife, Polly, with whom he had no children. James Wells grew up to be a strong and intelligent young man and was well treated by his father—but he was still a slave. He was sent by his father to Holly Springs to work as an apprentice with a carpenter who would teach him that trade.

James Wells was apprenticed to a Mr. Bolling, and it was in Holly Springs that he met a young slave woman named Elizabeth Warrenton, whom everyone called Lizzie. She had lived a more difficult life as a slave than James Wells had. She had been born somewhere in Virginia, probably around 1838. Elizabeth Warrenton came from a large family, and she along with several sisters, was sold to someone in Mississippi who sold them again. Apparently she had been beaten and otherwise mistreated as a child slave.

The second time Lizzie Warrenton was sold, Bolling, the carpenter in Holly Springs, bought her because she was an excellent cook. Slave owners such as Bolling often wanted their slaves to have children so that they could own more slaves. Legally, slaves were not allowed to marry in Mississippi, but some owners ordered slave marriages anyway. Bolling arranged such a slave marriage between James Wells and Lizzie Warrenton.

In the South of the late 1850s, agriculture based mainly on cotton was the major part of the economy, and slaves were a cheap source of labor, especially on the large farms called plantations. By 1860, many Americans, including some Southerners,

Unlike most slaves, who were agricultural workers, Ida B. Wells's mother was a cook and her father a carpenter.

opposed slavery and wanted to keep it from spreading as new states joined the growing Union. But Southern slave owners expected to be allowed to extend slavery to new territories and new states as the Union grew. The question of outlawing slavery in new territories was a hot issue in the U.S. Congress.

In 1860, Abraham Lincoln was elected President of the United States. He was closely identified with the people who wanted to end, or abolish, slavery. The rich white slave owners of the South feared that Lincoln would abolish all slavery so they began the move to secede, that is, leave, the Union. In January 1861, Mississippi, the state in which James and Lizzie Wells lived, joined other Southern states in seceding from the United States. These Southern states formed a new national government called the Confederate States of America. War between the Union states in the North and the seceded states in the South broke out a few months after Lincoln was sworn in as President in 1861.

Fifteen months after the beginning of the Civil War, James and Lizzie Wells's first child, Ida Bell Wells, was born in Holly Springs, Mississippi. When Ida was about three months old, President Lincoln announced that slavery would end in states still in rebellion at the start of the next year, 1863. Of course Mississippi, didn't consider itself part of the Union at the time he issued the Emancipation Proclamation. In this document, Lincoln stated "—I do order and declare that all persons held as slaves . . . shall be . . . free, and that the government of the United States, including the military. . . , will recognize and maintain the freedom of said persons." Fearing a bloody slave revolt, President Lincoln advised the former slaves to avoid "all violence . . . and I recommend . . . they labor faithfully for reasonable wages." Many of the slaves President Lincoln wanted free were still in areas controlled by the Confederacy. They were actually forced to labor for the Confederate Army, which was fighting the North. Others were forced to produce the goods that kept the South going during the war.

James and Lizzie Wells probably learned about the Emancipation Proclamation as the news was passed by word of mouth from slave to slave. Many African Americans fled toward Union Army lines knowing they would be free if they got to them, but others stayed where they were and continued working for their masters. James and Lizzie Wells, having a child, chose to stay where they were. After learning carpentry from Bolling, it was expected that James Wells would return to Tippah County once the apprenticeship was over. Then his owner could let others hire Wells for carpentry work and make money off the labor of his valuable slave. With a slave marriage such as theirs, it was likely that Lizzie Wells would stay with Ida in Holly Springs while her husband was sent away to work. Of course, as a small child, Ida didn't know how dangerous the times were. Her parents tried to give her a warm and loving home in which she was taught about the Bible and Christianity.

When Ida was less than three years old, the war finally ended. The North had won. But more than 600,000 people—more than half of them Southerners—had been killed in the brutal war. The South lay in ruins. The President's proclamation that slaves in states that had rebelled were free meant that there were almost 4 million newly freed African Americans, most without any way to provide for themselves. Many Southern factories, ports, cities, and railroads had been destroyed. Cotton production had fallen. Nearly 215,000 Southerners who had been prisoners of war returned to the South where food was often nearly impossible to find. The economy was so bad that a barrel of flour cost $1,000 in the old Confederate capital of Richmond, Virginia.

Clearly, the South had to be rebuilt, or reconstructed. The Reconstruction period lasted for 12 years, from 1865 until 1877. During the first few years after the Civil War, the South was divided into military zones over which the U.S. Army had control. Each Southern state had to ask to be readmitted to the Union it had left. In 1870, Mississippi was among the last four states to rejoin because each state first had to accept all the laws of the United States and the U.S. Constitution. Following the war years, the U.S. Constitution, which sets forth how the country is governed, had been greatly changed by three amendments. White leaders in Mississippi found it difficult to accept these three new amendments.

In 1865, the 13th Amendment had ended slavery in the United States. It made forced labor illegal except as punishment

This picture showing the hardships suffered after the Civil War also portrays the servantlike role for African Americans that many Southern whites hoped would continue.

for a crime, and it gave the national government power to make laws to enforce the end of slavery.

In 1868, the 14th Amendment was added to the Constitution. This amendment clearly made former slaves full citizens by declaring that any people who were born in the United States were citizens of both the United States and the state in which they were born. Further, no state could deny its citizens any rights granted by the United States. Specifically, no state could deny any citizens their life, liberty, or property without following "due process of law." *Due process* means following established legal principles in a way that protects the rights of the individual. The 14th Amendment further stated that no citizen could be denied "equal protection of the laws," so former slaves had to be protected just like any other citizen.

Two years later, in 1870, the 15th Amendment was passed. It declared that neither the United States government nor any state government could keep its citizens from voting because of their race, their color, or their having once been slaves.

These amendments to the Constitution were made necessary by actions in the Southern states. During 1865 and 1866, right after the end of the war, the Southern states passed new laws called Black Codes, which defined the rights and duties of the former slaves. These laws had forced African Americans to work according to yearly labor contracts and made idleness illegal. The laws also legally recognized earlier slave marriages but made marriages between Blacks and whites illegal. The Black Codes denied the right of Blacks to sue whites for violating their rights.

Mississippi had some of the strictest Black Codes in the South. Many of the old unfair laws dealing with the treatment and punishment of slaves were put into effect again, but the word *slaves* was replaced by the word *freedmen*. (Freed slaves, whether men, women, or children, were referred to as freedmen, throughout the nation.) African Americans in Mississippi could not even own farmland. Before reentering the Union in 1870, Mississippi had to end its Black Codes because these laws went against the three new amendments to the Constitution.

Once James Wells became a free man, he continued to work as a carpenter for Bolling for a couple of years, earning wages.

In the South, most African-American families continued to work as agricultural workers after the Civil War.

Then he got into a dispute with Bolling over voting rights. In 1867, black men had gained the right to vote in Mississippi. In fact, Mississippi was one of five Southern states where there were more black voters than white voters. When Bolling tried to tell Wells how to vote during an election, Wells refused to follow his instructions. Wells then moved his wife and family off Bolling's land into their own home where he earned his livelihood as a carpenter. Another thing that James and Lizzie Wells did as free people was to marry legally, even though slave marriages were now recognized as legal. (They had been *told* to marry as slaves; during the time of slavery, such marriages had not been legally recognized.)

James Wells's mother, Peggy, wanted her son to come visit, but his master-father's white wife, "Miss Polly," was still alive. James Wells thundered, "Mother, I never want to see that old woman as long as I live. I'll never forget the day she had you stripped and whipped the day after the old man [his master-father] died, and I am never going to see her.... [S]he could have starved to death if I'd had my say-so. She certainly would have if it hadn't been for you."

The Wells family continued to grow. Their second child was Eugenia. Next came three boys, James, George, and Eddie. The youngest of them, Eddie, died of an illness early in life.

Life in Mississippi was hard for most whites and former slaves, but some help did come from the national government and the North. In 1865, Congress had established the Freedmen's Bureau to help white refugees and former slaves adjust to life after the war. It supplied emergency food, clothing, and medical care. One of its most important functions was to help finance schools for African-American children. The Freedmen's Bureau often worked in cooperation with Northern relief agencies.

The freed people of Holly Springs, for example, were helped by a group of Northern white missionaries, the Freedmen's Aid Society of the Methodist Episcopal Church, who arrived shortly after the war ended in 1865. The following year, the missionaries set up a school named Shaw University. (In 1890, its name was changed to Rust College, which exists to this day.) Colleges are overseen by trustees, a small group of business and community leaders who are entrusted to run the college. Being asked to serve on a board of trustees is a major responsibility and honor, and it is thought that James Wells served on the first board for Shaw University. (Becauses of fires that destroyed the library and its contents twice, there are no records listing the first members of Shaw University's board of trustees, so there is no evidence beyond family remembrances that James Wells was on the board.)

James and Lizzie Wells clearly understood the importance of education; in most Southern states before 1865 it had been against the law for slaves to learn to read and write. Later in life, Ida explained the major job the Wells children had: "Our job was to go to school and learn all we could." Lizzie Wells joined her children at school long enough to be able to learn to read the Bible. Probably James Wells was too busy working as a carpenter to be able to go to school, but he often had Ida read him the news of the day. Small groups of his friends would come listen to his daughter read the news, and then they would discuss what it meant to them.

It was during these years that three more Wells children were born. Annie was born in 1873, Lily was born three years later, and in 1877, came the eighth and final child, Stanley.

The year 1877 was an important year for the South because it saw the end of the Reconstruction period. The last Union troops were withdrawn from Southern states. It was not surprising that many of the same wealthy white families that had ruled Mississippi before the war wanted to return to power. They resented the fact that voters had elected many local and state officials who were African Americans. One of Mississippi's U.S. senators was Blanche K. Bruce, the first African American to serve a full term as a U.S. senator. The ways of thinking that had brought on the Black Codes were still there, and many whites wanted to keep the former slaves "in their place."

Freed slaves had expected to be given land to farm after the war, but the national government soon set aside such plans. The Southern economy had relied on slave labor, which no longer existed. A new system took its place, with Blacks living nearly as they had as slaves. The whites who still owned the land rented it to Blacks to farm, and the rent was paid by giving the landowner a share of the crop. This was called sharecropping, and most African Americans in the South lived this way after the war.

The Wells family was more fortunate than most thanks to the carpentry skills of James Wells. They didn't have to live as poor sharecroppers did. With Shaw University in Holly Springs, the Wells children were able to go to school at a time when children were not required to attend school. In the rural South, girls were often able to spend more time in school than boys. Shaw offered classes at elementary and secondary school level as well as college courses. By 1877, Ida was taking college courses so she could become a teacher.

The Wells home was warm and protective of the children. On Sundays, Lizzie Wells would only allow the Bible to be read. The family often attended the church services of the white missionaries who had come to help with the school. Although Ida was becoming an attractive young woman, she was not allowed to date even at age 16. Her parents were strict and Ida's home life was secure.

Holly Springs was not an exciting place in which to grow up. In many ways it was a typical, small Southern town where people paid attention to each other's needs and looked out for the welfare of their neighbors. James Wells joined the Freemasons, a secret men's club that expects its members to help those in need.

The area around Holly Springs gets very, very warm during the long summer months. In the days before air conditioning, people left their windows open to keep their homes cool, and window screens weren't used. With so much warmth and a little standing water, mosquitoes could breed easily. And the South is famous for huge mosquitoes, which swarm at night.

Everyone knew what pests the mosquitoes were, but not even doctors knew they could spread a disease as they bit one person after another. About 25 miles from Holly Springs was the bustling port city of Memphis in the state of Tennessee. Huge ships from all over the world sailed up the Mississippi River to Memphis. If even one person on any of the ships carried the disease called yellow fever, all it took was one bite from a mosquito and the next person who was bitten by the same mosquito could be infected. More mosquitoes could become carriers of the disease by biting that infected person. Soon the disease could spread widely as the cycle of mosquito bites and infection continued. Because doctors didn't understand the role of the mosquito in spreading the disease, they didn't know how to stop it. An epidemic could result.

The name yellow fever comes from one of the disease's symptoms. Once bitten by an infected mosquito, a person could quickly get a high fever, and become very sick. Then the white parts of his or her eyes turned yellow as the disease became more serious. Often an ugly death followed—unlike today, when modern medicines can be used to cure the disease—and whole families could be wiped out in a matter of days.

During the summer of 1878, a yellow fever epidemic broke out in Memphis. In an attempt to stop the spread of the disease, homes in which it appeared were closed to outsiders. This practice, called quarantining, was even used for entire small towns when the disease was that widespread. A flag called a Yellow Jack was raised to warn outsiders of the danger.

The epidemic that started in Memphis was awful. Since the

only water for drinking came from shallow wells, it was not pure. The rapidly growing port town had no system for carrying away human waste, so dirty, infected pools of water surrounded the town. During the summer heat, the water in the river and the dirty pools gave mosquitoes the perfect place to breed.

On August 13, 1878, the first citizen in Memphis died from yellow fever. There had been a small yellow fever epidemic in Memphis five years earlier, so people knew about the disease. This time the epidemic was terrible. People fled Memphis to get away from it, but some of those fleeing were infected. They spread the disease through mosquitoes that bit them, and in this way, the epidemic spiraled out from Memphis. In less than a month, more than half of the 40,000 people who lived in Memphis had fled. Of the 19,000 who stayed, 14,000 were African

In Memphis, the yellow fever epidemic of 1878 wiped out whole families. The disease soon spread to Holly Springs.

Americans who mistakenly thought they could not get yellow fever. Making matters worse, among the people who fled Memphis were many doctors, so there was little care for the sick people who stayed behind.

The epidemic was so bad that the county coroner kept four furniture wagons working constantly just to pick up the dead. Coffins could not be made fast enough as the disease spread like wildfire. By the time the first frost in October had killed the mosquitoes and ended the epidemic, nearly 17,000 of the 19,000 people who had stayed in Memphis had been sick. And of that number, 5,150 people had died.

As the epidemic spread, the government of Holly Springs decided that, unlike some other towns, it would not be closed to people who were fleeing from Memphis. It was during this time that Ida visited her Grandmother Peggy in Tippah County where her father had been born. It seems unlikely that she was fleeing the epidemic, because the rest of her family stayed behind in Holly Springs. However, more than half of the 3,500 people in Holly Springs had decided to leave. The epidemic took an awful toll on those remaining in Holly Springs.

During Ida's visit to her grandmother's farm some neighbors from Holly Springs brought the terrible letter that told of her parents' death. It was three long days before another letter arrived, from a Dr. Gray, calling Ida home.

Ida's grandmother didn't want Ida to go, fearing that she, too, would become ill. But Ida could not be stopped. So many people had been fleeing from Memphis that passenger trains no longer ran toward the city and in the direction of Holly Springs. The only way Ida could get a train home was by riding in the caboose of a freight train.

CHAPTER TWO

Head of the Family

When Ida arrived back at her Holly Springs home, she learned that her baby brother, Stanley, had also died of yellow fever. He was only about nine months old. That left Ida with five younger brothers and sisters.

Dr. Gray, who was white, knew that the color of a person's skin had nothing to do with the good or bad qualities a person had. He told Ida what a cheerful and helpful man her father had been. Although yellow fever had broken out in his own home, Wells continued to use his skills for the sad job of making coffins. More than 300 people in Holly Springs died during the epidemic—nearly one person in every ten in the town. James Wells would come home to bring food and to check on the family's needs. But soon he also became ill and died. Dr. Gray told Ida, "Your father would be passing through the court house, which was used as a hospital, on his way to the shop, carrying some lumber to help make a coffin. If he passed a patient who was out of his head, he would stop to quiet him. If [the patient] were dying, he would kneel down and pray with him, then pick up his tools and go on with his day's work. Everyone liked him and missed him when he was gone."

The woman who stayed with the children until Ida got home was Dr. Gray's nurse. She told Ida, "That Dr. Gray sure loved your pa." Dr. Gray had sent her to look after the Wells children, and he continued to pay her just as if she were tending to the sick. She explained, "Dr. Gray sure is one good white man." Years later, Ida B. Wells recalled, "I never met Dr. Gray before or saw him again, but in all these years I have shared and echoed that nurse's opinion every time I think of his [Dr. Gray's] . . . watch over Jim Wells's family when they needed it."

Imagine how Ida must have felt! She had already lived through slavery, a terrible war, and the big changes of Reconstruction, and now she was responsible for five younger children. Her loving family and friends gathered around her, but Ida knew what happened to orphans, particularly if they were African American. Because there was no help from the state, and no way to provide for the children, various aunts and uncles would take the girls to raise as their own. The boys who were old enough would be apprenticed just as their father had been. Given James Wells's excellent reputation, there would be no difficulty getting them apprenticed. But Ida's sister, Eugenia, had a serious health problem. She had become severely physically disabled because her spine curved, doubling her nearly in two, making her unable to walk. Genie, as Ida called her sister, would have to go to the poorhouse where she would get very little care and no opportunity to improve herself. A poorhouse was where people with no money were sent to receive what little care society would give them. It would be a terrible place to live, especially for an African American with the problems Genie had.

Ida simply refused to have her family broken up. She must have stunned everyone when she announced that she would take care of them alone. It was unheard of for a 16-year-old schoolgirl, with an ill sister and four other younger children, to do that. But she would have it no other way. Dr. Gray helped Ida get the modest amount of money that her parents had managed to save. With her new responsibility to the children, the youngest of whom was two years old, Ida could not continue in school and graduate from college. But many teachers in those days did not have college degrees. Besides, at this time it was unusual for an African American to have any college training.

The Freemasons, the secret men's group James Wells had joined, helped Ida apply for a teaching job in a small country school about six miles outside of Holly Springs. Ida knew the small savings her parents had left would provide for them until money from her teaching came in. The school year was shorter than it is today, with the months in school being the time of year when children wouldn't be needed to help with the farmwork. The children Ida taught were probably the sons and daughters of sharecroppers.

During the Reconstruction years many people in the South

could not read. Typically one-third of all Southerners, and two-thirds of all African-American Southerners, could not read at all. On the other hand, for the first time many African-American children had the chance to go to school. During the Reconstruction years, tax-supported free public schools for blacks and whites were set up in the South. Although by 1876 most Southern states required some sort of tax-supported public schools, no laws required parents to send their children to school. Teachers were seldom trained how to teach because it was assumed that people who could read and write could teach others how to do it, too.

Ida got the teaching job, which only paid $25 a month—at a time when a skilled worker such as a carpenter earned from $31 to $49 a month—but it was enough to keep the family together. Also neighboring sharecroppers were generous with vegetables, eggs, and dairy products for the family, and that was very helpful. Getting to school was difficult, however, because she had to ride on a mule to get there. So she could only come home on weekends

The Freedmen's Bureau and missionaries helped set up more than 1,000 schools to teach freed people to read and write.

to wash and iron and to check on the children, particularly Genie. After working all weekend at home, she would ride the mule back for another week of teaching. It was a hard life for a young woman. Her aging grandmother moved in to help with the children because Ida couldn't be home as much as she needed to be.

The effort to keep the family together took its toll on everyone. Ida's grandmother soon suffered a stroke and was no longer able to care for the children. Genie's health got worse and worse. Ida spent the two years until she was 18 putting all her efforts into teaching and keeping the Wells family together.

Now that she had experience and had proven herself as a teacher, Ida B. Wells began looking for another, better-paying teaching job. When she managed to find a better job, it was across the Mississippi–Tennessee state line, in Shelby County. The city of Memphis is in Shelby County, but there were two separate school systems for the city and the county. Because Memphis was wealthier than Shelby County, it paid teachers more. Ida B. Wells's real aim was to get a job in the city schools. But the position in Shelby County was a good step up. Her first job was at the Woodstock School, where she taught elementary-school children.

Some other arrangement, however, had to be made now for her brothers and sisters. Ida Wells's main concern was Genie. Fortunately, their mother's sister, Belle, offered Genie her caring and loving home. Aunt Belle lived on a farm, so she also took the two boys, who were able to earn their keep by helping with the farmwork. Another aunt, Fannie Butler, had lost her husband in the yellow fever epidemic, but she offered to take the two youngest children into her home. In 1885, Fannie Butler moved with her three children and Annie and Lily Wells to Visalia, California.

With the family taken care of, Ida Wells moved to Memphis. She used the Chesapeake, Ohio, & Southwestern Railroad to get back and forth from her home in the city to her work in the county school. She was willing to pay for a first-class seat in the "ladies' car" so that she wouldn't have to ride with smokers, liquor drinkers, and other people with whom she did not want to associate. The people, whether white or black, who bought the

Head of the Family

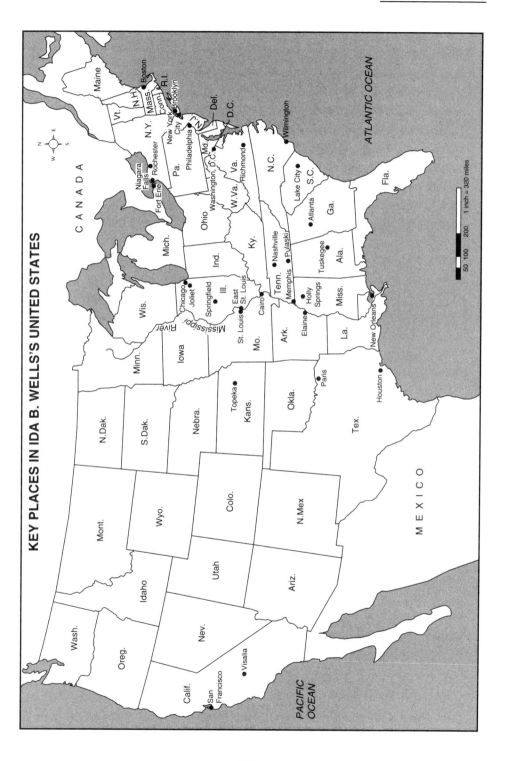

tickets for the more expensive first-class train coaches preferred those cars to the less expensive "smokers." For Ida B. Wells, riding in the ladies' car was certainly quite a change from riding a mule to work!

One of the events that shaped Ida B. Wells's life occurred while riding one of those trains. Many people used trains daily throughout the nation, and they sat close together as they rode. The same people who in the 1860s had supported the Black Codes now wanted to separate people of different races on trains among other places. After Reconstruction ended in 1877, white-controlled governments in much of the South began to allow more and more discrimination against African Americans.

A number of court cases dealt with whether the United States government had the right to tell individuals or private companies not to discriminate against people of other races in their private conduct. These cases challenged the Civil Rights Act of 1875. In that Reconstruction law, Congress had prohibited all *persons* from practicing certain forms of discrimination. The law said that people could not deny, on the basis of race, any individual's equal use of hotels, public transportation, theaters, and other public places. This 1875 federal law had clearly applied to private conduct.

In 1883, the U.S. Supreme Court, the highest court in the country, delivered its opinion on these civil rights cases. The Court ruled that the U.S. government could not limit *a person's or a business's private conduct*, even if that conduct restricted the use of public places. The Court said that Congress could prevent *state governments* but not individuals or companies from interfering with civil rights.

According to this Civil Rights Cases decision of 1883, Congress did not have the power to prevent a person from using force to block another person's right to vote in state elections or even to attend public schools. Such actions would supposedly be against state laws. But they would not violate the national government's 14th Amendment, which provided for "equal protection of the laws." Only such discriminatory action by a state government might go against the U.S. Constitution. This U.S. Supreme Court decision reopened many of the issues that had been at the heart of the old Black Codes. It also opened the door for a new series of state and local laws, called Jim Crow laws. These were designed to reduce the rights and freedom of African Americans. Throughout the South schools were routinely divided between schools for Blacks and schools for whites. Doctors' offices and many churches were also segregated in the same way. Many white Southerners were looking for additional ways to increase segregation. Passenger trains were a natural target.

No doubt Ida B. Wells had read about the 1883 Supreme Court decision. Nevertheless, she continued to ride first class on the train. After all, in 1881 the state government in Tennessee had made it illegal to charge African Americans for a first-class ticket and then give them second-class seating. Tennessee laws also required that railroads in the state provide separate first-class seating for Blacks that was of equal quality to that which was provided for whites.

As in other Southern states, the state government of Tennessee was trying not to violate the 14th Amendment to the U.S. Constitution while at the same time permitting the segregation of African Americans. But since 1883, when the Civil Rights Act of 1875 had been declared unconstitutional (meaning it could not be enforced), the states did not have to worry if private companies, such as the railroads, violated African Americans' civil rights. After the 1883 Supreme Court ruling, states were more free to limit the civil rights of former slaves. Segregating Blacks from whites took many forms: besides separate schools and separate waiting rooms in doctors' offices, there were separate public rest rooms. White nurses were not allowed to attend to African Americans. Even the cutting of hair was segregated. Some factories had separate entrances for white workers and black workers. (By then Jim Crow laws supporting segregation had spread across most of the South.)

But back in May 1884 Wells had yet to personally experience the Jim Crow laws. She was well established as a teacher in Shelby County Schools, and the train ride from Memphis to her school and back was routine.

One May morning, Ida B. Wells bought her usual first-class ticket and headed for the ladies' car in which she had so often been seated. As usual, the ticket agent came along checking passengers' tickets. He asked Wells for hers, which she handed to him. The agent said he couldn't take her ticket and returned it. Wells assumed that the agent simply didn't want it and resumed her quiet reading.

A few minutes later the ticket agent returned and told her to leave the car. That meant giving up the first-class seat she had paid for and going to the second-class smoker car, which she didn't want to do. She later explained: "He tried to drag me out of the seat, but the moment he caught hold of my arm I fastened my teeth to the back of his hand." That must have been some bite! The agent, rubbing his hand, went for help because he couldn't handle Wells alone. Three men then came and ordered her to leave. The men were cheered on by the white women in the car who wanted Wells to leave. She explained that "some of them even stood on the seats so they could get a good view and continued applauding the conductor for his brave stand."

The "brave" men finally pulled Ida B. Wells from her seat as she struggled with all three of them. When the train arrived at the next stop, the men removed her from the train. As it chugged off, there at the station stood the schoolteacher looking rumpled and with her coat sleeve torn, but still holding her first-class ticket!

But the Chesapeake, Ohio & Southwestern Railroad had not heard the last of Ida B. Wells. She decided to take the railroad to court. The first lawyer she hired was an African-American attorney from Memphis who unfortunately took a bribe from the railroad not to proceed with her case. She then hired a white lawyer who took the case to a Tennessee state court. The judge, a former Union soldier, ruled in Ida B. Wells's favor. The railroad had broken the 1881 Tennessee law against charging for a first-class ticket but providing only second-class seating for African Americans. It had also broken the law by not providing black passengers with a first-class coach with accommodations equal to those provided for white passengers. The judge ordered the railroad to pay the unusually high sum of $500 in damages. That was at a time when the average yearly earnings of a nonfarm worker totaled about $445.

Ida B. Wells had not heard the last of the Chesapeake, Ohio &

Southwestern Railroad though. The local press had a field day reporting her story. Even newspaper audiences were segregated based on their racial viewpoint. White readers of the *Memphis Daily Appeal* saw a headline that read: "Darky Damsel Obtains a Verdict for Damages Against the Chesapeake & Ohio Railroad."

That may have been the first time that Ida B. Wells read about herself in a newspaper. However, it would be only the first of many times that she would make the news.

CHAPTER THREE

Getting Established in Memphis

Winning her case against the Chesapeake, Ohio & Southwestern Railroad Company did two things for Ida B. Wells. She had $500 (less the court costs and her lawyer's fees) to put in the bank. And she had shown the confidence to stand up for what she thought was right.

Wells started making plans to get a teaching job in the Memphis city school system. She studied hard for the teacher's exam and reflected on what she had learned during her first years of teaching. At the beginning of the 1884-85 school year, she got the Memphis job, which meant higher pay and easier traveling to get to and from work. It also introduced her to many exciting people in Memphis.

The city of Memphis must have been a great place for someone who had grown up in a small town. Wells once described herself as "a green girl"—inexperienced—when she was in her teens. The library at Shaw University had opened the world of books to her. In addition to the Bible, she had read works by Charles Dickens, William Shakespeare, and Louisa May Alcott, so she was fairly well read. But she was aware she had never read any books about African Americans or any works written by them.

In Memphis, she started having contact with other African Americans. She joined a lyceum, a group that presented educational and cultural programs such as concerts and lectures. Lyceums were popular in cities like Memphis in the days before radio, TV, and motion pictures. Wells's lyceum group was mainly made up of other African-American schoolteachers. In addition, she took private lessons in public speaking and drama. These lessons were of great importance to her later in life.

It was also in Memphis that Ida B. Wells first had contact with the AME (African Methodist Episcopal) Church. It had been founded in Philadelphia, Pennsylvania, 100 years earlier by

Richard Allen, a former slave who had purchased his own freedom. The AME was closely associated with the Methodist Church and was open to all, although its membership was mostly African American. It focused on missionary work and education, so it was natural for Ida B. Wells to join.

Through her new friends in Memphis, Ida B. Wells met the Reverend R. N. Countee, who published a religious newspaper called the *Living Way* once a week for African Americans in Memphis. He encouraged her to submit a letter about her train experience and court case for the paper to publish. Her letter in the *Living Way* was well received, having both a powerful message and a simple, direct style. It was the first of many letters she published in it. As was fashionable in those days, she didn't sign her own name to her letters. She used what is called a pen name. For unknown reasons, she chose the pen name "Iola."

Wells had adopted the popular practice of writing a daily diary. Her January 5, 1886, entry sounds like someone getting over the flu after winter school vacation: "School reassembled yesterday. I now have three classes. The *Living Way* came out Saturday with my letter in it. Taught today, feeling worse than I have in some time; my chest & head have been in an uproar all day." Her diary didn't indicate that this start on her career as a journalist and writer was any more important to her than getting over a case of the flu.

Reading and writing were very important activities during the 1880s and 1890s. Printing presses became common, paper was cheap, and people wanted to know the news of the day. Most people did not have telephones, and radios had not yet been invented. The news was sent by telegraph; reporters could use it to send news stories great distances quickly. With hundreds of thousands of African Americans taking advantage of schools and learning to read, hundreds of independent African-American-owned-and-operated newspapers for African-American readers sprang up across the United States. That made the contributions of black writers important.

Although the U.S. Constitution guaranteed American citizens certain rights, living under Jim Crow laws made it an empty guarantee. The power of custom in the South, supported by the Jim

Crow laws, led white Southerners to expect every black American to stand, hat in hand as a mark of respect, and to address every adult white person no matter what his or her status, as "Sir" or "Ma'am." At the same time, such whites called any young black adult "boy" or "girl" and older ones "uncle" or "aunty." The use of such labels constantly reminded Blacks that whites thought that black citizens were inferior to any white citizen.

Wells was not well suited to living under Jim Crow laws—or with anyone telling her what to do or how to act. She could be fiery, stormy, and independent when necessary. She wrote in her diary for January 13, 1886: "Thursday was city election day; I was not interested in anything but the School Board [which was elected] & both colored men were beaten; we now have an entirely white Board." Her entry speaks well for Memphis merely because African Americans were at least *allowed* to run for the school board, and it indicates that black citizens were still allowed to vote there. In much of the South, Jim Crow laws were taking the right to vote away from the former slaves. While the *right* for African Americans to vote was clearly spelled out in the 15th Amendment to the U.S. Constitution, being *allowed* to vote was certainly another matter.

Ida B. Wells's feelings about the rights of African Americans were deeply rooted. She never forgot the slavery and segregation lessons taught to her as a child, so she had to question the segregation she now witnessed. An interesting entry in her diary demonstrates both her belief and her questions: "February 8 [1886]: . . . I had intended on retiring [going to bed] early in order to arise soon enough to attend the Moody [one of America's most famous preachers of the day] and Sharkey [Sankey, a hymn writer] meeting Sunday morning. We got a front seat in the gallery. He . . . tells the simple truth that Christ Jesus came on earth to seek & save . . . I intended writing Mr. Moody asking him why ministers never touch on that phase of sin—the caste distinction—practiced even in church." By *caste*, she meant the dividing of a society into classes based on birth, wealth, religion, or race. Here she says that it is a sin to divide people purely because they are white or black. Membership in her AME church was largely African American, after all, although it was open to everyone.

Another diary entry a little later described a case in which a white man had beaten a black woman, and when he tried to abuse her further, she beat him. For that she was sent to the workhouse—a jail where she was put to work on a chain gang. Nothing was done to the white man who started the trouble to begin with. Wells clearly didn't think this was fair.

Her diary also reveals that there were other interests in her life. One was teaching and another was stylish clothes! She was better paid in Memphis, but a teacher's salary was still low. Making matters worse, from time to time the school board ran out of money and she sometimes had to wait months to be paid. With money tight, it was hard for the oldest sister to send money to her brothers and sisters, but she continued to think about them. Ida B. Wells's struggle to keep the family together created a loving warmth that time and distance could not end. Although her sister Genie had died, Wells was able to see her two brothers who lived nearby. Her two youngest sisters in California were too far away to visit. She longed to see them again.

Wells knew that one way to improve her income was to be qualified to get a better job. So she enrolled in summer school at Fisk University, in Nashville, which was more than 200 miles away. (Fisk University had been started by members of the American Missionary Association and General Clinton Fisk of the Freedmen's Bureau of Tennessee, among others.) Wells was taking courses that might enable her to become a school principal. All the while, however, she continued to write for an increasing variety of African-American newspapers. Her topics involved cases in which African Americans were badly treated because of segregation, ignorance, and racial hatred.

Wells had started teaching without completing formal training. She was also not formally trained as a journalist. But increasingly, her articles were reproduced in other African-American newspapers and she was often quoted by other writers. She was asked to contribute to and edit the *Evening Star*, the lyceum's publication, and she was approached for additional work by the *Little Rock Sun*, the *Detroit Plaindealer*, and other newspapers. She found herself torn between teaching, writing, and family responsibilities.

Wells found the opportunity to visit her sisters Annie and Lily and her Aunt Fannie Butler in Visalia, California, when the National Education Association (NEA) held its national meeting in July 1886 in Topeka, Kansas. Being a teacher allowed Wells to buy a discount railroad ticket to attend the meeting. She saved enough money to get from there to California. While at the conference, she was struck by how few African-American educators attended. She explained in her diary: "Had a fine time in Topeka. Met many teachers from different parts. Such crowds and crowds of people! I never saw so many teachers in my life. About 30 are of our race." Even as she wrote those words, her mind must have drifted to California. By July 29, she reached San Francisco, the city whose bay opens directly onto the Pacific Ocean. She went to the famous Cliff House, which perches atop cliffs fronting the huge Pacific. It was the first time she had ever seen an ocean. She also agreed to be interviewed for an article by the *Elevator*, the African-American newspaper printed in San Francisco.

But the main objective of her trip had been a family visit, not new adventures. She headed south and was in Visalia early in August 1886. It had been eight years since the deaths of her parents and baby Stanley. Annie was now 13 and Lily was 10. But Aunt Fannie looked old and tired. Wells wrote in her diary: "Poor Aunt F.! She wants me to stay the year with her whether I get any work to do or not & I, seeing how careworn she is with hard work . . . know she is right & I should help her share the responsibility."

It must have been a difficult visit for 24-year-old Wells. Visalia held her loving and tired aunt and her two youngest sisters. Should she stay with them and teach there if she could find a job? There were, however, other job offers in San Francisco, Kansas, and Memphis.

Wells was about to take a teaching job in Visalia. But she learned that the African Americans in the town had asked for a separate school for their children. The one-room school they were given was in no way equal to the school the white children went to, and Wells refused to teach in it. She was angry that African Americans wanted to be separate, and she later wrote an article describing the situation: "There was not a separate school in the State of California until the colored people asked for it. To say that we want to be to ourselves is a tacit acknowledgment of [a quiet agreement with the idea of] the inferiority [of African Americans] that they [whites] take for granted anyway." Torn as she was, Wells chose to return to Memphis for the next school year. It was a fateful decision.

Once again she was caught up in current events. After reading a story about an African-American woman who had been brutally murdered in Jackson, Mississippi, Wells wrote a fiery article about it. She explained in her diary: "Wrote a dynamite article . . . almost advising murder! . . . A colored woman accused of poisoning a white one was taken from the county jail and stripped naked and hung up in the courthouse yard and her body riddled with bullets and left exposed to view! O my God! can such things be and no justice for it? . . . It may be unwise to express myself so strongly but I cannot help it." Her hatred of discrimination and violence against African Americans was moving her in the direction of a career in journalism.

Memphis continued to be an exciting place for Wells to live. The busy port of Memphis had seven railroads leading into it, and it was a major cotton market, so there was always something new going on. The town was growing rapidly. It had also become the fifth-largest grocery market in the United States. Also, it was 44 percent African American, and Wells enjoyed living in the growing African-American community.

She also returned to the lyceum and church group activities—and her continuing case against the Chesapeake, Ohio & Southwestern Railroad. The railroad company appealed the outcome of the trial to higher courts. By now Wells knew that the $500 for damages didn't matter to the railroad. But the fact that an African-American woman was able to win damages for trying to use a ticket she had legally purchased could weaken a Jim Crow law. And that mattered a lot to segregationists!

CHAPTER FOUR

Finding a Cause

Wells was a young woman of 24 when she returned to Memphis in September 1886. By this time her life was becoming centered around a circle of friends and her teaching career. While she, like all African Americans, felt the sting of segregation in Memphis, it really was beginning to feel like home to her.

Knowing that she had been offered teaching positions on her trip to California must have given Wells a sense of personal security. Although she wanted to teach older children, she had never been given a class higher than fourth grade, and she was now realizing that her heart wasn't fully in teaching. This was in marked contrast to the success she had realized as the journalist "Iola" and her enthusiasm about writing.

Wells began the 1886-87 school year as she had all the others before. But in the spring, she learned the Tennessee Supreme Court had overruled her earlier victory against the Chesapeake, Ohio & Southwestern Railroad Company. Having the victory overturned made Wells furious. She felt that she had won the $500 in damages fairly, but there was more at stake for the company than just the $500. Years later she found out that her case had been the first in which an African American had successfully gone to a Southern state court since the Civil Rights Act of 1875 had been declared unconstitutional in 1883. Her legal victory would have broken a string of white court victories that dated back to before the end of Reconstruction. She explained: "The success of my case would have set a precedent [become a model] which others would doubtless have followed. In this, as in so many other matters, the South wanted the Civil Rights Bill repealed [withdrawn] but did not want or intend to give justice to the Negro after robbing him of all resources from which to secure it." The end of Reconstruction meant that matters of civil rights and equal protection of the law would be left up to the state court systems rather than United States, or federal, courts. In the South, most judges did not believe African Americans were really entitled to such rights.

Wells was very bitter over the court ruling. She had turned to the state of Tennessee and expected its laws to protect her from being abused for simply riding on a train and using the ticket she had paid for. This decision by the Supreme Court of Tennessee had been appealed as high as possible given that a Tennessee state law was being challenged, so there was nothing else to do. It wasn't the last time that Ida B. Wells would feel the courts were unjust.

Her diary provides an interesting insight into the court case and its real meaning to African Americans. She wrote: "I feel so disappointed, because I had hoped such great things from my suit for my people generally. I have firmly believed all along that the law was on our side and would . . . give us justice. I feel shorn [deprived] of that belief and utterly discouraged . . . now if it were possible I would gather my race in my arms and fly far away with them. O God, is there no redress, no peace, no justice in this land for us?"

Disappointed with the courts, she turned to her writing for the press to speak out about injustice to African Americans. Her writing was powerful, driven by a belief that justice was denied to many African Americans simply because they weren't white. To Wells, writing was a way both to vent her anger and to better conditions for African Americans; she didn't think of it as a way to make a living. Her newspaper columns were often reprinted in other papers and enjoyed by those in the African-American community who knew she was right in her call for equal rights for all. But she was also upset by the lack of support for her among some African Americans in Memphis.

Meanwhile, Wells continued teaching, working in the AME Church, and enjoying the lyceum. Perhaps because she had given up so much of her own youth to her family, she was not a person who made friends easily, yet she knew many people. She had made one close friend in Betty Moss, whose husband, Thomas, was a postal worker in Memphis when Ida first met them. The Mosses were a hardworking couple who wanted their daughter,

Maurine, to have more than they had. Ida liked this couple and soon regarded them as her best friends. Obviously, they felt the same way about her because they asked her to become Maurine's godmother. That was a great honor. A godparent was expected to adopt and raise the child if anything happened to both parents and there were no family members to care for the child. But what could possibly happen to such a nice young couple? Tom Moss talked about someday buying a grocery store so he could have his own business. His friends with whom he shared that dream, Calvin McDowell and Henry Stewart, became Ida B. Wells's friends, too.

Sometime in 1889, Wells's writings in the *Living Way* moved the Reverend Taylor Nightingale, pastor of the Beal Street Baptist Church, the largest African-American church in Memphis, to offer her a job working for his paper, the *Free Speech–Headlight*. Her reaction told a lot about her character. She liked to work *with* people, not *for* them. So she said she would only accept the offer if she was a partner. She bought one-third of the paper, whose title was later shortened to the *Free Speech*, and became its editor as well as part owner. She still was not thinking about making journalism her profession, but it was a move that made her writing all the more important.

For the next two years, Wells continued teaching for the Memphis city schools while working as editor for the *Free Speech*. The name of the paper was appropriate, for she felt free to comment publicly any time she thought an African American was being denied a civil right.

She had plenty to write about. Most Blacks in Memphis lacked the power and income of many whites. However, there was a growing middle class of educated African Americans. Some African Americans practiced a profession, such as teaching or the law, whereas others owned businesses. No matter what their education or occupations were, however, many whites looked on them with prejudice because of their race and slave backgrounds. African Americans suffered from discrimination, which is behavior that is unfair to any member of a particular group, simply because they are members of that group. Many whites thought that Blacks were a lower race and that "all of them looked the same anyway." African Americans suffered from this stereotyping by whites who held the incorrect belief that all members of a group have the same qualities or act the same way.

But hateful words and the Jim Crow laws were only some of the many evils African Americans faced after the end of Reconstruction. One of the most serious problems was that their right to vote was being taken away. Once that happened, how would they ever gain the other political and civil rights guaranteed to all Americans? How could they make further progress if laws could be passed without their concerns being taken into consideration?

African-American men had been guaranteed the right to vote by the 15th Amendment in 1870. (There was as yet no amendment guaranteeing the right to vote to women of any race.) Through voting during the Reconstruction period, African Americans had elected many local and state officials. But many white political leaders in the South were working hard to make sure that black citizens would not have political power for long.

Each state had the power to decide the rules for voting by its citizens. That meant the right to vote could be taken away at the local and state levels. Throughout the South, different rules were used to deprive African-American people of their voting rights.

One of the most effective ways of taking away African Americans' rights was by terrorism, the systematic use of violence by a group in order to force others to give in to its demands. Some whites organized hate groups against Blacks. The worst among these was the Ku Klux Klan (KKK). Whites had started the KKK in Pulaski, Tennessee, less than 200 miles from Memphis, when Ida B. Wells was only five years old. It began as a kind of secret army that opposed the Reconstruction government of Tennessee. It was soon dedicated to the use of violence to keep African Americans "in their place." The Klan, as it was called, quickly spread all over the South, particularly where the number of Blacks was nearly as large as the number of whites. Members of the Klan hid their faces behind white sheets, using violence and terror against Blacks and their white supporters.

The 19th-century Klan had reached its peak membership in the late 1860s and early 1870s. By the 1880s, its goal of white

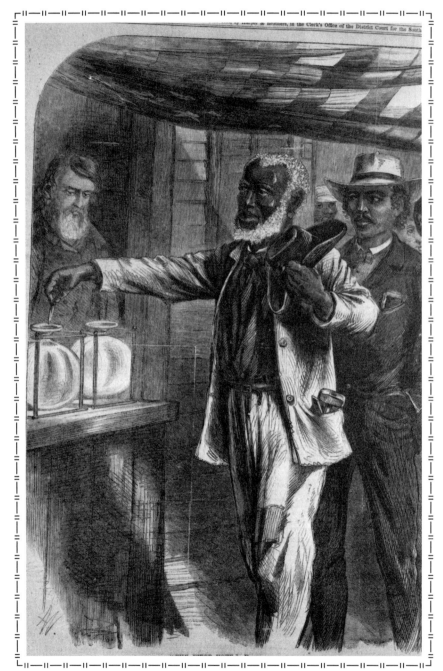

Freedmen voting for the first time in 1867. In 1870, they were guaranteed voting rights by the 15th Amendment.

supremacy had been achieved in most places in the South. Although Klan membership rapidly declined in the 1880s, a climate of fear and violence remained in many places.

In such an atmosphere of fear, most journalists would have been careful about what they wrote, but not Ida B. Wells. There was too much segregation and hate in her world to be ignored. For example, African-American men and women were frequently described and stereotyped as stupid, lazy, and only interested in sex. Wells knew that simply wasn't correct. Her own diary refers to her concern that one of the young men she dated might actually try to kiss her! She hardly sounded like the loose, wicked woman in the stereotype!

Wells used the *Free Speech* to speak out on a number of controversial issues. She attacked whites who stereotyped Blacks. She wrote articles against dishonest politicians and other powerful men in the community, even if they were African Americans. She also denounced African-American men who sided with whites against Blacks for their own gain. In particular, she criticized African-American political leaders who did not press the federal government to protect the civil rights of black Americans. And she wrote several articles about the important but often ignored roles of women in history.

After two years on the paper she wanted to call attention to the segregated Memphis schools in which African-American children were placed. The idea that *all* school children ought to go to school was being accepted in the North. Called compulsory attendance, meaning required attendance, the idea had not yet caught on in many parts of the South. School boards had a hard time getting enough money for the schools, even without making all children attend them.

One way to provide better schools for whites was to pay black teachers less, hire less qualified teachers, put black students and teachers in poor buildings with fewer supplies, and even make the school year shorter for black children than that for white children. In the South, many African-American children had to work in the fields alongside their parents. Their families could not afford to hire workers to take the children's place while they were in school. Many white Southerners showed little interest in spending money to educate African-American children anyway. It was against these practices utilized in the Memphis school system that Ida B. Wells spoke out about in 1891.

As a teacher in Memphis, Wells knew that she had to be careful concerning what she said about her employer. Nevertheless, she wrote a very critical article about the lack of concern for African-American students in the Memphis schools. Then she approached the Reverend Taylor Nightingale about signing the article for her. The African-American churches had great power in the black communities throughout the South, and Nightingale's Beal Street Baptist Church was the largest in Memphis, so the minister could influence many people by signing the article. Hundreds of copies of the *Free Speech* were sold in his church each week.

To Wells's surprise, he wouldn't sign it. Rather than withdraw it, she let the *Free Speech* print the article with her own name attached. It was widely read, and then the white newspapers condemned it. As a result, she became a target of much white hatred. At the end of the 1891 school year the Memphis school board fired her. Even though she had thought this might happen, Wells was stunned. After all, she had taught for seven years in Memphis.

What really shocked Ida B. Wells was the lack of support from members of the African-American community. She explained: "Of course I had rather feared that [firing] might be the result; but I had taken a chance in the interests of the children of our race and had lost out. The worst part of the experience was the lack of appreciation shown by the parents. They simply couldn't understand why one would risk a good job even for their children. The burden of their simple refrain was, 'Miss Ida, you ought not to have done it; you might have known that they would fire you.'"

The parents' reaction clearly showed how powerful the fear of white reaction had become among African Americans. When one person stood her ground, others didn't dare to join her. But Wells wasn't content to "get along" in such a system; she wanted to fight it!

Wells clearly knew that fighting the system could be dangerous. Within a week of having her railroad case overturned by the

The reading public saw one of its first pictures of Ida B. Wells when this engraving was printed in 1891.

Tennessee Supreme Court in 1887, she had written in her diary: "Have just returned from what I consider to be the best thing out. The Negro's Mutual Protective Association had a public meeting. . . . I was very much enthused as I listened to the speeches and the earnestness of the men present. The Negro is beginning to think for himself and find out that strength is to be found only in unity." That call for unity was one that she would echo for the remainder of her life. After all, if African Americans would unite in their calls for justice and equal rights, they would be stronger as a group than as individuals and they could stand up against the hate groups they often confronted.

Having lost her teaching job, Wells seemed to have no immediate alternative but to become a full-time journalist. She needed to earn a living, and her investment in the *Free Speech* gave her the job she needed. So she went on the road into areas outside of Memphis selling subscriptions to the newspaper and getting stories for it at the same time. But it was an unusual role at that time because she was one of very few women news reporters doing this sort of work. After all, what she was doing was considered "man's work," but she was as opposed to prejudice against women as she was opposed to prejudice against African Americans. In about nine months, she was earning as much as a journalist as she had earned as a classroom teacher in Memphis. Plus, she had found out how much she really loved being a reporter.

In her new full-time job, Wells was in and out of Memphis often. Nevertheless, she kept up with her friend Betty Moss and her godchild. She must have been really proud of Thomas Moss, who along with his friends Calvin McDowell and Henry Stewart, had combined their money to buy a small grocery store, just as Thomas and Betty Moss had dreamed.

Having planned for so long, Thomas Moss and his friends had wanted to open a store where they felt sure they could do well. They had found an area right on the streetcar line in a neighborhood that was largely African American. The streetcar, or trolley, was the most commonly used public transportation in Memphis; that meant that people could easily get to their store and back home. They named the store the People's Grocery Company.

Finding a Cause

Thomas Moss was a caring father and a hardworking man. He kept his job at the U.S. post office, working days delivering the mail. After a full day's work walking his route, he went to the People's Grocery to work for several more hours.

Nearby they had a competitor—a white-owned grocery. With all the segregation in Memphis, African Americans didn't feel welcome at the white-owned store. Besides, the prices there were higher. The white owner, W. H. Barrett, was angered by the competition, which threatened his business. Now that there was another place to shop, most African Americans avoided Barrett's store, but legally there was little he could do. Since he was losing his customers to Thomas Moss, Barrett threatened the People's Grocery, claiming that a white mob could attack the store. Moss checked with the police to see what kind of help could be expected. Because the grocery was just beyond the Memphis city limits at a place called "The Curve" on the trolley line, there was little help available. Moss, his friends, and others from the area had to protect the store themselves. They armed themselves against any violence. The competition between the two stores continued.

Accounts about what happened next vary widely. That is understandable because the white press explained the situation in a way that made whites feel justified, and the black press reported events differently. Based on any account, something awful happened.

While details are unclear, it is known there had been some type of crime committed around the grocery, and a group of whites charged Moss and his partners with it. Some reports said the real crime was being "too successful" and "uppity." Others reported that Moss and the others were charged with raping a white woman, something such a good family man seemed unlikely to have done. In any event, a group of nine deputies, wearing street clothes and not uniforms, was sent to serve a warrant at the People's Grocery. For some reason, the deputies apparently entered through a back door where they were fired on by the African Americans there to protect the store. Three deputies were wounded, but Moss and his friends stopped firing as soon as they realized they were shooting at deputies. A total of 30 African-American men, many of whom had been protecting the grocery, including Moss, McDowell, and Stewart, were arrested. The grocery had to be closed because the owners couldn't be there. But with the public enraged, not even the jail was a safe place to be.

On the night of March 9, 1892, shortly after the owners of the People's Grocery were jailed, a group of white men disguised as deputies entered the jail, seized them, and then dragged them away from the jail. No one can know what horror Thomas Moss, Calvin McDowell, and Henry Stewart faced during their last minutes alive. They were badly beaten, shot several times, and finally hanged, left dangling in the wind without ever having a chance to defend themselves in court. No charges were filed against the killers, and no one was ever punished for the brutal and senseless murders. Perhaps if there had been charges, and the accused were put on trial, proven guilty, and punished as they should have been, then lynching like this might have been stopped.

Lynching is an old and brutal practice. In it, people who are accused of a crime are put to death without the normal legal process to determine guilt. In the past, the members of a mob

An engraving, showing a man about to be lynched. By the 1890s, one such lynching occurred every three days.

that lynched someone were almost never punished, and charges were almost never filed against the lynchers. Most lynch victims are beaten, tortured, mutilated, burned, shot, or hanged alive by an angry mob without any trial to determine if the accused are guilty or not. In some cases, however, convicted criminals have been pulled from jails and murdered. In the United States, lynchings were recorded as early as the Revolutionary War, a period when the law favored the British. In the 20 years before the Civil War, more than 300 people are known to have been lynched, and fewer than 10 percent of them were African Americans. At that time, most African Americans were slaves and therefore valuable property.

After the Civil War was over, white terrorist groups like the Ku Klux Klan turned to lynching to "keep the colored in their place," which meant, among other things, not being more successful in business than whites. In the 80 years from 1882 to 1962, 4,736 people were reportedly lynched in the United States, 3,442 of them being African Americans (nearly 73 percent of the total). By the 1890s, lynching reached its peak of one lynching about every three days. It had become so common that beginning with the 1883 New Year's Day issue of the *Chicago Tribune* and for the next 21 years, the newspaper listed the lynchings and where they had occurred during the preceding year.

In the spring of 1892, Ida B. Wells was only months away from turning 30, but her life changed drastically after the murder of Thomas Moss and his friends. She was now a woman with a cause: Lynching of innocent African Americans simply had to stop. What she needed was a way to make the cause known.

CHAPTER FIVE

Beginning the Crusade

Ida B. Wells was in Natchez, Mississippi, more than 200 miles away from Memphis when she learned of the lynching of Moss, McDowell, and Stewart. She was on one of her frequent trips, selling subscriptions to *Free Speech* and searching for news stories. She hurried home but arrived too late for the funeral.

These brutal lynchings were out of character for the people of Memphis. There had been a violent riot there in 1866, following the end of the Civil War. The 1866 riot came in response to efforts of some whites to register Blacks to vote. But nothing like these lynchings had happened before. The city was usually preoccupied with its growth. In 1892, Memphis became the only city south of St. Louis, Missouri, with a railroad bridge across the Mississippi River. That bridge made going west easier for people. It also meant that huge amounts of material came to Memphis by river and rail to be loaded onto the stream of railroad cars that headed west. In the 20 years between 1880 and 1900, the city's population increased from 33,000 to 102,000. By 1900, nearly half that population was black. Among the white population, only 2 percent had been born in Memphis; all the rest had moved into the expanding city. By then, it also had a modern city water system and sewage system, making life easier and healthier for its citizens. Such a growing city needed hard workers, not racial hatred.

By the time Wells got home to her best friend and her godchild, even more senseless violence had occurred. The African-American community in Memphis was horrified and angry over the brutal murder of three good men. In shock, African Americans gathered near the People's Grocery. Many in the group spoke angrily about the lynching and said they would tolerate no more of it. But they did nothing more.

When word reached the white leaders of Memphis that a

number of Blacks had gathered at the People's Grocery, they feared a riot might start. The sheriff was ordered, as Wells later reported, "to take a hundred men, go . . . and shoot down on sight any Negro who appears to be making trouble." To shoot anyone who *appears* to be making trouble? Memphis was a city that was emotionally charged, with the black community and the white community full of hate and fear of each other. What actually arrived at the People's Grocery was a white mob, not a police force. During the short, bloody clash that followed no one was killed, but many people were injured. Members of the white mob then broke into the People's Grocery, taking what they wanted and, out of pure hatred, smashing other things.

The white grocer had won. The People's Grocery owners were dead and the store ransacked. What little was left was later taken to pay the bills for the food the owners had bought to supply the store. It must have been unbearable for Wells to look at her best friend, widowed, expecting a child, and completely broke. The lynchings were acts that simply could not be allowed to go unnoticed and unpunished.

One lone woman would have a hard time fighting the whole city of Memphis. Nevertheless, Wells used the two weapons she had available to fight back: her mind and her voice through *Free Speech*.

First, Wells needed to know as much about the lynching as possible. By reading news stories and talking to people she found out that Thomas Moss had begged for his life because of his family, and his last words apparently were: "Tell my people to go West—there is no justice for them here."

Wells repeated Moss's words in the next issue of *Free Speech*: "There is nothing we can do about the lynching now, as we are out-numbered and without arms. . . . There is therefore only one thing left we can do; save our money and leave a town . . . [which] takes us out and murders us in cold blood when accused by white persons." Unfortunately, no copies of *Free Speech* are known to still exist, but the story was carried in many other African-American newspapers.

A war of words followed. The white press of Memphis reported how awful the African Americans of Memphis were. The *Free*

Speech continued to report acts of racial hatred. Wells's investigation of recent lynchings throughout the South showed that there was a pattern to many of them: A white woman would claim that an African-American man had raped her, and an angry crowd would gather. Rather than wait for a trial and a chance to see if the charges were accurate, the mob would grab the African American and brutally kill him. In some cases, *any* African American was grabbed to satisfy the mob's thirst for blood. Wells had started what would become a lifelong crusade against the lynching of African Americans who were denied the protection of law. This former slave was becoming a powerful voice for the rights of African Americans.

Wells urged Blacks to boycott white-controlled businesses in Memphis. So African Americans stopped using the trolleys and stopped buying in white-owned stores. It did little to calm the nerves of anyone in Memphis.

With the level of hatred between Blacks and whites growing, the idea of moving west was taking hold among many African Americans. Who could possibly want to live where leading newspapers openly called for violence against people just because of their race? The *Free Speech* continued to advise African Americans to go west, as Thomas Moss, right before his death, had urged them to do. Leaving Memphis was possible in part because of the opening of Indian Territory to settlers in 1889. By 1890, that area had been organized as Oklahoma Territory. Although the U.S. government permitted land to be taken away from Native Americans, settlers saw this as a chance to own good land on which to farm. Many African Americans from Memphis took this opportunity also. (In 1907, Oklahoma became a state.)

Wells explained the westward movement: "Every time word came of people leaving Memphis, we who were left behind rejoiced. Oklahoma was about to be opened up, and scores of people sold or gave away property, shook Memphis dust off their feet, and went out West as Tom Moss had said for us to." Wells visited Oklahoma Territory as a reporter for *Free Speech* and spent several weeks traveling by train, interviewing people who had left Memphis, and seeing what life was like there. Her weekly reports from Oklahoma Territory for the *Free Speech* clearly

Ida B. Wells with her friend Betty Moss and Moss's two children about a year after Thomas Moss had been lynched.

encouraged others to move from Memphis. She finally left Oklahoma Territory because of earlier plans to attend an AME church conference in Philadelphia. The trip north gave Wells a chance to think about where to move *Free Speech*, because she, too, had decided it was time to leave Memphis.

While on her trip to the conference, Wells's newspaper, *Free Speech*, published an article prepared before she left. It continued the ongoing war of words by reporting the following on May 21, 1892:

> Eight Negroes lynched since last issue of Free Speech five on the same old racket—the new alarm about raping white women. The same programme of hanging, then shooting bullets into the lifeless bodies, was carried out to the letter. Nobody in this section of the country believes the old thread-bare lie that Negro men rape white women. If Southern men aren't careful, they will overreach themselves and public sentiment will have a reaction; a conclusion will then be reached which will be very damaging to the moral reputation of their women.

What "conclusion" the article was referring to was that some of the white women who claimed they were raped by black men were actually having voluntary and longtime relationships with black men. White supremacists who might ignore relationships between black women and white men became enraged when it was pointed out that similar relationships existed between white women and black men.

Within days, on May 25, both the *Daily Commercial* and the *Evening Scimitar*, the leading white Memphis newspapers, reacted strongly to the article in *Free Speech*. The *Evening Scimitar* took a violent stand, saying, "Patience under such circumstances is not a virtue. If the Negroes themselves do not apply the remedy without delay, it will be the duty of those whom he [the writer of the unsigned *Free Speech* article, apparently assumed by whites to be a man] has attacked to tie the wretch . . . to a stake at the intersection of Main and Madison Sts., brand him on the forehead with a hot iron, and perform upon him a surgical operation [castration] with a pair of tailor's shears."

While this battle of words continued in the press, reporters from many African-American newspapers were covering the AME national conference. As the only woman editor in Philadelphia, Ida B. Wells was the center of attention. She met T. Thomas Fortune, the famous editor and part owner of the *New York Age*. Fortune had often reproduced her columns in his paper and had written to her about her work. Fearing that the outspoken Wells would be in danger if she returned to Memphis, he strongly suggested that she stay out of that city.

His advice was wise. More violence was breaking out in Memphis. A group of whites met at the central meeting place in Memphis, the Cotton Exchange, where large bales of cotton were sold for shipment down the Mississippi River to ports all over the world. These men didn't want thousands of African Americans to continue to leave Memphis because they were losing a dependable source of cheap labor. And they hated the loss of business caused by the continuing boycott of white businesses by Blacks. On May 27, 1892, they focused their anger on the militant voice of the African-American community. As a mob, they marched on the *Free Speech* offices. Fortunately the business manager and part owner of the newspaper, J. L. Flemming, learned the mob was coming just in time to escape. In its fury, the mob broke into the building, smashed office furniture, wrecked the lead type used to print the news, and tore the building up. They left a note warning that anyone who attempted to print the *Free Speech* again would be lynched.

Wells was traveling hundreds of miles away in New Jersey where she had agreed to meet Fortune following the church conference. As she got off the train, he greeted her with the news about the destruction of the *Free Speech*. Ida B. Wells described her reaction this way:

> Although I had been warned repeatedly by my own people that something would happen if I did not cease harping on the lynching of three months before, I had expected that happening to come when

> I was at home. I had bought a pistol the first thing after Tom Moss was lynched, because I expected some cowardly retaliation by the lynchers. I felt that one had better die fighting against injustice than to die like a dog or a rat in a trap. . . . I felt that if I could take one lyncher with me, this would even up the score a bit.

Wells was clearly a woman on a crusade. Her courage had cost her the newspaper of which she was part owner, but its loss only put more fire into her crusade. She was quickly assured that Flemming was all right, and then she wondered about her own fate. She had invested everything in the paper, so she had lost a great deal. But she had not lost her concern for the African Americans of Memphis. It was obvious that Wells wasn't afraid for her own life, but what effect would her return to Memphis have on other African Americans there?

Wells knew it was not safe for her to return to Memphis. But it was her voice that had to be heard defending innocent people, speaking out against lynching, and demanding civil and political rights. T. Thomas Fortune took advantage of the situation and offered her a position on the staff of the *New York Age*. For Wells, the offer represented a chance to continue doing exactly what the mob that had wrecked the *Free Speech* offices thought they had finally stopped. Now, however, she had a nationally circulated newspaper in which to tell the truth about the horror and hate that were so common in the lives of African Americans in 1892.

Ida B. Wells had a crusade, a national audience, and an important story to tell. The horror and bigotry of lynching continued, but finally there was someone in a position to make the nation aware of it. But would that be enough?

CHAPTER SIX

On the World Stage

It didn't take Ida B. Wells long to make herself heard in the *New York Age*. She barely had time to move from Memphis to New York City and get settled in her job before she published her story on June 25, 1892. In a lengthy, seven-column feature entitled "Exiled," Wells told about "lynch law" and the murder of Thomas Moss and his friends plus her own story of the destruction of her newspaper. The term *lynch law* refers to a mob dealing out its own justice—lynching—without waiting for the legal system of laws and courts to determine if the person is guilty. Wells had long wondered why people in the North didn't say or do anything about the way the African Americans were treated in the South. She assumed they simply didn't know about it.

Her story was powerful because it was written by someone who had been a victim herself. She explained, person by person, charge by charge, crime by crime, the pattern of lynch law. She had never believed the "old threadbare lie" that a white woman couldn't be attracted to a man of color. If there was no such attraction, how could anyone explain what Wells called the "bleaching" of her people? During slavery it had not been at all unusual for a white male owner to have a child with a black slave woman. Her own father, James Wells, had been the result of such a situation. Yet white men refused to admit that a white woman could have the same interest in a black man. This simply didn't make sense.

Wells studied reports about lynching throughout the South. Time and again she found that African-American men were charged with stealing, rape, or sometimes simply not being respectful toward whites. The pattern was for a charge to be made without any witnesses; that accusation whipped up a mob of whites who either captured the victim themselves or simply dragged the poor soul out of jail—with the law-enforcement officers normally doing nothing to stop them. The mob would then beat, brand, humiliate, and finally kill the victim with no trial, no justice, and no pity. And no one was charged with any wrongdoing after committing such brutality.

The *New York Age* was a widely read newspaper among African Americans in the North. But with Wells's story in it, 10,000 copies were printed, and 1,000 alone were sold on the streets of Memphis. To African Americans in Memphis, it showed that Wells would not stop. To the white community, some of whose members had ransacked her office and threatened her, it was a victory for the woman they wanted to silence. The white press lashed out at her, calling her a liar and troublemaker.

The reaction was no less than what she expected. She explained:

> It seemed horrible to me that death in its most terrible form should be meted [handed] out to the Negro who was weak enough to take chances when accepting the invitations of these white women; but that the entire race should be branded as moral monsters and despoilers of white womanhood and childhood was bound to rob us of all the friends we had and silence any protests that they might make for us.

The power of Wells's story was felt by all who read it. Among the readers was the famous African-American abolitionist, writer, and diplomat Frederick Douglass. In his 75th year, Douglass was impressed with what he read. He realized the importance of Wells's work because of his own background. Having been born a slave, he had escaped to the North, and at the age of 24, he had started lecturing about slavery's evils. After Douglass had begun writing about slavery, he had been forced to flee to England so he would not be hunted down by his former owner and returned to slavery. In 1847, he had started his own newspaper, crusading against slavery and for the rights of women. Naturally, as he read his copy of *New York Age*, he was interested in the author of the article "Exiled."

As a young man and escaped slave, Frederick Douglass spoke out against slavery.

Wells's article showed that in only about a third of the lynchings was the victim accused of rape and that in these incidents the charge was false most of the time. Yet the idea that real crimes of rape were what brought about most lynchings—and therefore perhaps justified them—was believed by most white Americans and even many African Americans.

Douglass had been so moved by Wells's article, that he came to see her. He was aware of the growing number of lynchings but not how widespread the practice was. Wells quickly became a close friend, visiting Douglass and his second wife, Helen Pitts Douglass, whenever she could. The Douglasses were particularly aware of racial prejudice because Helen was white. Many African Americans were either uncomfortable around them or ignored Helen even when visiting in the Douglasses' home. Frederick Douglass explained to Wells. "Well, my dear . . . I am not criticizing them. I am only trying to tell you why we enjoyed your company so much and want you to come again." Her response was typical: "I certainly deserve no credit for what I have been taught is ordinary good manners. The fact that Mrs. Douglass is white had nothing to do with it."

The friendship between Ida B. Wells and Frederick Douglass began because of a mutual hatred of prejudice and grew with the respect they had for each other. Perhaps Douglass saw some of his youthful vigor and hatred of injustice in young Wells. Over the next few years, Douglass was willing to write articles and letters for Wells when she needed the support of his name.

Not all Northerners welcomed Wells's message. One of the largest and most powerful newspapers in the country was the *New York Times*. Wells expected that large, white-read Northern newspapers such as the *New York Times* would carry her story and shame the South into stopping the crime of lynching. On September 4, 1892, the *New York Times* carried a story about the Executive Committee of the New York State Cleveland League, which it called "an organization of colored Democrats." It reported that the executive committee had lashed out at Wells. The president of the organization had said: "Regarding Ida Wells, I speak for the honest and intelligent masses of my race when I call her a fraud. . . . She knows nothing about the colored problem in the South. We all regret that lynchings occur there, but we approve of them to the extent that the white people of the South do." As ignorant as his words were, the fact they were reported in the *New York Times* foretold two problems Wells would face: an uncaring white press and African Americans in the North who would not respond to her calls for justice.

Among those who read and remembered Wells's lynching story were two women, Victoria Mathews of New York and Maritcha Lyons of Brooklyn. They succeeded in raising enough money and attention to have Wells come to New York's Lyric Hall on the evening of October 5, 1892. The hall was filled to capacity as people came to hear "Iola" speak.

This was the first time that Wells, for all of her written words, had been called on to deliver a formal speech before a large crowd. Speaking to a group frightens many people, so it was not unusual that she, too, was nervous. She had written out what she wanted to say, but the message and the audience upset her. Tears began to flow as she bravely read on. No doubt her tears only made the horror of lynching all the more real to the audience. Despite the tears, she finished the speech, which obviously moved the audience. A collection was taken up, and Wells was given $500 to put in the bank to help her start her own paper again. She was also given a small pen-shaped pin, as the symbol of her work. She would wear the pin proudly for many years.

Most important, the women of the then separate cities of

New York and Brooklyn understood what they needed to fight for. So the first African-American organization of its kind, the Women's Loyal Union, was formed. The goals of this women's club were to protect and extend the rights of African Americans and women.

The October 6 *New York Times* did not even report her speech of the previous night. However, a few weeks after Wells had spoken, the demand for copies was such that a version of it, a pamphlet entitled *Southern Horrors: Lynch Law in Its Phases*, was reproduced by the *New York Age* and sold for 15 cents a copy. At the front of the pamphlet was a copy of a letter from Frederick Douglass to Ida B. Wells in which he wrote, "Brave woman! you have done your people and mine a service which can neither be weighed nor measured. . . . It seems sometimes we are deserted by earth and Heaven—yet we must still think, speak and work, and trust in the power of a merciful God."

In her own modest way, Wells explained in her preface to *Southern Horrors*, "It is with no pleasure that I have dipped my hands in the corruption here exposed. Somebody must show that the Afro-American race is more sinned against than sinning, and it seems to have fallen upon me to do so." Then, in the 20 or so pages of the pamphlet, she simply reviewed case after case in which an African American, usually a man although sometimes a woman, was dragged from jail or home by a mob. There could be anywhere from 10 to 100 angry people in the mob, some hiding their shame behind masks, some not. But the result was the same as they stole the role of judge, jury, and law, to brutally murder people who couldn't defend themselves. Using a phrase that was common, she referred to "Judge Lynch" and the lack of justice.

Wells's powerful words were hated by some members of the white-owned press, which frequently lashed out at her. Early in 1893, she hired two African-American attorneys, Ferdinand L. Barnett and S. Laing Williams, to investigate suing a newspaper that had attacked her. While the lawsuit was unimportant, later the interesting and attractive Ferdinand L. Barnett became far more than her attorney.

But the word of Wells's powerful speech soon spread to other women, who were forming political groups of their own. Wells was invited to speak in many cities and towns including Philadelphia, Washington, D.C., and Boston. It was in Boston that she had her first opportunity to address a white audience on the horrors of lynching. Many who heard that address wanted to know more about these crimes against African Americans.

On February 4, 1893, the day following a speech by Wells in Washington, D.C., the newspapers were filled with reports about a particularly brutal lynching in Paris, Texas, a small town about 75 miles northeast of Dallas. An African American in Paris was accused of having raped and then murdered a four-year-old girl. He was caught and dragged to jail, and plans were carefully made to torture him slowly before finally killing him. Incredibly, neither the Paris nor the Texas government did anything to stop this carefully planned murder. Schools were closed, special trains ran from neighboring towns, and thousands of people came from all over to see the lynching. Great care was taken to make his death as slow and as agonizing as possible. And of course, no trial was held. No witnesses were called. No rights were given to this human being who died a death as horrible as the sick minds who planned it could create. He was beaten, kicked, burned with hot irons, and humiliated for hours before being burned alive while the crowd celebrated. Lynching was not new in Paris. In 1886, people in the Texas town had lynched a white man who was accused of killing a deputy sheriff. His death was far less violent, however.

Wells later recalled the event this way.:

> The [African-American] man died protesting his innocence. He had no trial, no chance to defend himself, and to this day the world has only the word of his accusers that he had committed that terrible crime. . . . For that reason there will always be doubt as to his guilt. There is no doubt whatever as to the guilt of those who murdered and tortured and burned alive this victim of their blood lust. They openly admitted and gloried in their shame.

In another horrid example of lynching, an African American

On the World Stage

A brutal lynching. In lectures and in writings, Ida B. Wells took the lead in demanding an end to all lynchings.

named Ed Coy was burned alive by a mob that included the white woman he was accused of raping. A judge later concluded that she had been a willing participant in her relations with Coy, yet she was the one who lit the fire that burned the man alive!

Newspapers around the world reported the lynchings. Across the Atlantic Ocean in England and Scotland, the lynching report was read by horrified people. Among them were Isabelle Mayo and Catherine Impey, who were both actively involved in fighting segregation in India. Mayo asked Impey why Americans were so cruel. In discussing the matter, Impey said that she had heard Wells's speech in Philadelphia and, in fact, had met her. Mayo asked Impey to contact Wells and ask her to come to Great Britain to deliver lectures on the lynching problem. Their organization would pay her costs.

Getting an invitation to speak in England and Scotland was very important to the antilynching cause. In 1893, the British were major investors in the United States, and Great Britain was a huge market for American goods. Wells continued to be frustrated by the lack of interest in the North about stopping lynching, so she thought that maybe an appeal to the British market would receive some results. Certainly what she said about lynching while in England and Scotland would receive a great deal of coverage in newspapers around the world. Wells explained how it felt to receive the invitation:

> It seemed like an open door in a stone wall. For nearly a year I had been in the North, hoping to get the truth [about lynching to the people] and get moral support for my demand that those accused of crimes be given a fair trial and punished by law instead of by mob. In only one city—Boston—had I been given even a meager hearing, and the press was dumb [silent]. I refer, of course, to the white press, since it was the medium through which I hoped to reach the white people of the country, who alone could mold public sentiment.

With the encouragement of Frederick Douglass, Ida B. Wells

accepted the invitation. After all, the 1892-93 world's fair, called the World's Columbian Exposition, was being planned in the United States, and the eyes of the world would focus on it. So American business and pride could both be appealed to. What better time to call attention to the crime of lynching?

On April 5, 1893, Wells left for Great Britain. Nearly a year had passed since the senseless murder of Thomas Moss and his friends. The trip took nine days on the rough Atlantic. Not surprisingly, Wells got quite seasick. It is safe to assume, however, that she had plenty of company. The ship docked at Liverpool, on England's west coast, the second largest port in the country. Catherine Impey met her and took her home for several days' rest. Then they went north to Aberdeen, Scotland, to meet Isabelle Mayo. They had a lot in common. Mayo's work against segregation in India made her politically active as both an organizer and a writer. The network of interested groups Mayo had established was anxious to hear from a black American about why some Southern whites took the law into their own hands and brutally killed defenseless people.

For several weeks Wells and her new British friends toured the larger cities of Scotland and England speaking to interested groups about the horrors of lynching. Often the press attended her speeches, and the news reports appeared on both sides of the Atlantic. Predictably the Southern white press ridiculed Wells, questioning why she was speaking out on this matter in England and Scotland. The British press was much more complimentary, and she left having helped start the Society for the Recognition of the Brotherhood of Man. That group's goal was to end separation of the races.

When Wells returned to the United States in June 1893, she found the white-owned Northern press still largely quiet about her crusade. Of great concern to her, once again, was the lack of support from the African-American community. So Wells again toured Northern cities, attacking the continuing violence in the South. She simply couldn't ignore a practice that butchered an average of 100 African Americans a year during the 1880s and 1890s. The previous year had been the worst: 161 lynchings were reported in 1892 alone.

The 1893 World's Columbian Exposition. Wells wrote a pamphlet protesting against discrimination at this Chicago World's Fair.

Before Wells went to Great Britain in 1893, her attention had turned to a problem developing in Chicago. The year 1892 was the 400th anniversary of Columbus's arrival in America. For several years, a giant world's fair had been planned for 1892 and 1893 to celebrate that historic event. It was to be a great opportunity to show the tremendous progress that had been made since 1492. Many countries had exhibits in buildings called pavilions. Chicago was the site of this world's fair, called the Columbian Exposition. It focused the world's attention on Chicago, where the latest scientific discoveries were displayed. As part of the world's fair, for example, the first electric trolley system in the United States was built.

A world's fair meant that hundreds of new jobs were created, but almost no African Americans were hired for them. African Americans were also excluded from the exposition's programs about American progress. Upon Wells's return to the United States in 1893, she sought the help of her former attorney, Ferdinand L. Barnett, who was also the owner and editor of the *Conservator*, one of the most influential African-American-owned newspapers in Chicago. Wells recruited Ferdinand L. Barnett and Frederick Douglass to join her in speaking about this issue at African-American churches in Chicago. She hoped that in this way they could raise enough money for a pamphlet to hand out to visitors at the world's fair. The pamphlet would protest not only the lack of jobs for African Americans but also the fact that they were not represented on the programs or in the displays. To a visitor at the Columbian Exposition, the impression given was almost as if there were *no* African Americans in the United States.

The amount of money raised from the African-American community for the pamphlet was disappointing, but there was enough to print 20,000 copies of *The Reason Why the Colored American is Not in the World's Columbian Exposition*. The free pamphlets were given out at the Haitian pavilion. (The Haitian pavilion was a meeting place for many African Americans visiting the world's fair since there were no major African-American exhibits.) The 81-page pamphlet included sections written by Douglass, Wells, and Barnett. Wells stayed away from some of the events at the Columbian Exposition but continued to speak out in churches against discrimination.

Although protesting discrimination at the world's fair, Wells was involved in many other activities in Chicago. She loved cultural events like the theater—Chicago had several—and evening entertainment such as the symphony orchestra. Chicago was basically a new city, having suffered a huge fire in 1871 in which much of the city had been burned to the ground. As Chicago was rebuilt, a carefully planned and modern city was created. Neither the trolley system nor the schools were segregated, and Chicago had a well-established African-American population with a growing middle class. It seemed like a place Wells could call home.

While staying in Chicago in 1893, Ida B. Wells also organized some of the city's leading African-American women into a club that met weekly for lectures and other cultural events. She had

Ida B. Wells

Ida B. Wells carried her antilynching campaign to Northern cities and, on two lecture tours, to Great Britain.

seen such clubs in New York, Boston, and other cities. Within a year, members named their group the Ida B. Wells Club, the first African-American women's club in Chicago.

Perhaps in frustration over the lack of organized response to her antilynching campaign in Northern cities, following the world's fair, Wells returned to her friends in Great Britain in mid-1894. This time she was employed by a white-owned newspaper, the *Chicago Inter-Ocean*, as its first African-American writer. She agreed to send back to the newspaper letters about her European trip. The series of letters appeared in a column entitled "Ida B. Wells Abroad."

Again she was greeted with interest and curiosity as she toured Great Britain. Most people would have been exhausted from the pace she maintained, but at age 32, Wells still burned with her crusade against lynching. While in England, Wells got into a major dispute with Frances Willard, president of the National Woman's Christian Temperance Union located in the United States. Willard was also a founder of the World's Woman's Christian Temperance Union and was at that time living in England. Willard's position as head of the largest women's organization in the United States made any disagreement with her serious. Because both the National and the World's Woman's Christian Temperance Unions campaigned against public bars and alcoholic drinks, the moral importance of the organizations was significant. In addition, Willard worked for getting the right to vote for women, so she also had political support, especially among women.

Willard had given an interview in 1890 in which she made unfavorable remarks about African Americans in general and, some thought, about Wells in particular. Her published comments had enraged Wells, who quoted some of them in an article in Great Britain. The dispute between Wells and Willard was widely reported, with white-owned Southern newspapers often supporting Willard and Northern newspapers siding with Wells. Finally, Frances Willard took a stand against lynching. But the Southern branches of the Woman's Christian Temperance Union remained segregated. The disagreement between Wells and Willard gave wider coverage to the lynching issue, which is what Ida B. Wells wanted.

CHAPTER SEVEN

Torn Between Family and Cause

Ida B. Wells returned from Europe to Chicago on an August day in 1894. Members of the Ida B. Wells Club greeted her at the Chicago train station. As was the custom in her travels in Great Britain and the United States, she stayed in the home of a club member. Her Chicago hostess was Mrs. A. H. Brown, who made her very much at home. Wells quickly realized how worn out she was from her almost constant travels, so she planned to stay for at least a month.

Her second trip to Great Britain seemed to have brought about some immediate results. Within a month of her return, Congressman Henry Blair of New Hampshire called for the federal government to investigate previous acts of violence such as lynching. Although Blair presented petitions against lynching sent from citizens of several states, including some from the South, the U.S. House of Representatives did not vote to start such an investigation. Nevertheless, more people began to speak out against lynching. Several states, such as North and South Carolina, Georgia, Ohio, Kentucky, and Texas, even passed anti-lynching laws. These laws, however, were not strictly enforced. Wells's native state of Mississippi and her adopted states of Tennessee and Illinois still had no such laws. In the late summer of 1894, six African Americans were accused of burning barns and were lynched in the Memphis area. This time, Memphis business leaders and white-owned newspapers at least condemned the local lynchings, but the lynchers were not convicted.

Once back in Chicago, Wells was able to devote a bit more time to her personal life. She was a beautiful, intelligent, and cultured woman, and she had always been particular about her appearance. Since her days as a teacher in Memphis, her diary shows that she bought attractive, stylish clothing. Although she enjoyed the company of young gentlemen, Wells loved her independence. Years before, in Memphis, she had written in her diary on Valentine's Day, 1886: "Mr. G. & I had a bout [fight] last week. He renewed his question . . . if I could tell him I 'cared for him' without a like assertion [statement] on his part. He seems to think I ought to encourage him to speak by speaking first—but that I'll *never* do. It's conceding too much and I don't think I need buy any man's love. I blush to think I allowed him to caress me."

Her diary reveals her deeply religious and proper upbringing. On May 6, 1886, she had written: "Had a talk with G. . . He called that evening and asked me to kiss him, but I gently but firmly refused." At that time there were no telephones in Memphis, so the reference to a "call" meant that he came by. It was common in those days to refer to people by their initials—such as "Mr. G."—in case anyone snooped in one's diary.

Ida B. Wells had explained the problem of being an unmarried and attractive young woman to her diary, in the middle of June 1886: "My affairs [activities] have always been at one extreme or the other. . . . Just now there are three in the city who, with the least encouragement would make love to me; I have two correspondents [people she writes to] in the same predicament. I am an anomaly [someone unusual] to myself as well as to others. I do not wish to be married but I do wish for the society of gentlemen." By the following February, she may have started rethinking her relationships with men, for she wrote that "Vickie O. was married last week. I am the only lady teacher in the building who is unmarried."

Until she came to Chicago, Wells had probably remained that "anomaly" she had written about several years earlier. Once she was back after her 1894 trip to Great Britain, she again saw the attractive Ferdinand L. Barnett. He was a successful attorney and part owner of the *Conservator*. Barnett was, himself, active in the African-American community and very much opposed to segregation. He also had political ambitions. There was something special about this refined and dignified widower with two small boys, Ferdinand, Jr., and Albert. Ida B. Wells slowly rethought the idea of not being married.

Ferdinand L. Barnett had been born into slavery in Nashville, Tennessee, in 1856. When he was three years old, just before the

Civil War started, Barnett's father bought his family's freedom and moved them to Canada where slavery was illegal. In 1869, a few years after the war was over, the family moved to Chicago. Barnett graduated from Northwestern University with a law degree in 1878, the same year Wells's parents died in the yellow fever epidemic.

In late 1894, Ida and Ferdinand decided to get married. But Wells insisted that first she would make a major lecture tour of the cities in the North and West. She planned to speak against lynching again and to charge a lecture fee. The money earned would help pay for her travel expenses and the cost of a new book she was writing. Ferdinand agreed to postpone the wedding until the next year.

Wells conducted her lecture tour and wrote a new antilynching booklet. Clear and forcefully written, *A Red Record* laid out the story of American lynching for all to see. On the pamphlet's cover sheet she dedicated her work this way: "Respectfully submitted to the Nineteenth Century civilization in 'the Land of the Free and the Home of the Brave.'" Using the last line from "The Star-Spangled Banner" this way, she made it very clear that for African Americans living at that time in the South those were still hollow words.

In 100 pages she listed three excuses used to justify lynching: the need to control race riots, the concern that African Americans could become an organized voting force, and finally the "threadbare lie" that white women couldn't be attracted to black men. Then she explained the scope of Southern lynching. Using 1893 as an example, she listed the reasons for which African Americans were lynched, including 39 for rape, 13 for related suspicion of intent to rape, 44 for murder, 11 for near murders, and a list of other things such as 2 for "well poisoning," 1 for "wife beating," 2 for "insulting whites," 4 for "unknown offense," and 1 for "no offense," and 4 for "racial prejudice." The total came to 159. Further, she listed the offenses by state, with Alabama leading with 25, followed by Georgia with 24, and concluding with 1 each in Indian Territory and New York State.

The statistics were shocking. Wells then filled page after page with the details of individual lynchings, including such vicious acts as the lynching of two children (whose father had been charged with murder), after which their father was lynched. Another case detailed how an African-American man who had been charged with killing a baby had been tortured in unbelievable ways. The lynched man's stepson was then lynched for no reason—even though the boy had nothing to do with the supposed crime. She explained that another man was lynched because a jury had found him innocent! Other cases included lynchings for being "saucy" to white people, for writing a letter to a white woman, for proposing marriage to a white woman, and for no reason at all—"without cause." The leading charges continued to be rape and attempted rape.

The pamphlet was widely distributed in the United States and Great Britain. *A Red Record* stunned those who read it. But still the Northern press and African Americans were largely quiet and unresponsive.

Even getting married came in second to Wells's crusade against lynching. The wedding was scheduled twice, only to be put off while she gave yet another speech. Finally, on June 27, 1895, Ferdinand and Ida were married in an elegant wedding. No attention was wasted on the race of those who attended. When there was no family member in Chicago to host her wedding, the Ida B. Wells Club asked to fill in. At a time when women were denied the right to vote, Wells had helped organize the first Illinois Woman's Republican State Committee, and the committee asked if its members could attend the wedding. As Wells explained: "These women did attend in a body, accompanied by their husbands, and were dressed in honor of the occasion in evening attire, just the same as if they had attended a wedding among themselves." It was good to be recognized for the woman she was without race being a consideration.

Wells sent for her two sisters from California, who were bridesmaids for this special occasion. So many people attended the wedding of these two well-known people that the street in front of the church was packed; it was nearly impossible for Wells's coach to get her to the church on time. While "Make Me Thine Own" was played on the organ, Ida B. Wells and Ferdinand L. Barnett were married. Their lives were changed forever.

Ida decided to keep her birth name as well as her husband's name. She was now Ida B. Wells-Barnett. She had at first expected to come home after the honeymoon and settle into the quiet, secure life of a housewife and mother. A week after the wedding, however, Ida was running the *Conservator*, which she had bought from Ferdinand and his business associates. She began working as a journalist again.

Several events in 1895 and 1896 had major effects on African Americans and on the direction of her own life. In February 1895, Frederick Douglass, the great African-American abolitionist, publisher, reformer, writer, lecturer, and diplomat, died. After the Civil War, he had been a leader in the fight for civil rights for African Americans. Douglass had also been a strong supporter of the women's rights movement and of human rights at home and abroad. With the death of Douglass, many African Americans turned to Booker T. Washington as their new leader.

Booker T. Washington had been born into slavery in Virginia in 1856. He grew up in great poverty and worked as a boy in salt furnaces and coal mines. He studied at the Hampton Institute and Industrial School. Later he became head of a new school in Alabama called the Tuskegee Normal and Industrial Institute. He developed the Tuskegee Institute from a few shacks with one teacher and about 40 students to become one of the most important African-American educational institutions in the world.

Washington's major concern was defining the role of African Americans in American society. Because most African Americans came from poor farm families, he emphasized the learning of craft skills and industrial and farming methods. He stressed that African Americans should improve themselves by making themselves better workers first. They should learn the value of good work habits, thrift, and cleanliness. He urged African Americans to get a good practical vocational education rather than study the liberal arts in college.

Washington also thought African Americans should avoid demanding their full civil rights, including the right to vote. Instead of fighting discrimination and segregation, they should work at becoming economically secure. He believed that African Americans should not challenge whites directly and should not

Booker T. Washington with leading industrialists and philanthropists. Wells criticized his stand on civil rights.

demand to be treated equally. He feared it would be too risky for African Americans to demand political rights until they were better off economically. According to Washington, in time—once Blacks had become economically powerful—whites would respect and accept them. Gradually African Americans would gain political rights and power.

In September 1895, Washington gave an important speech presenting his ideas to an audience of Blacks and whites at the Atlanta Exposition in Georgia. He said, "In all things that are purely social we can be separate as fingers, yet one as the hand in all things essential to mutual progress." White business leaders welcomed this message of self-help and self-improvement for African Americans, as well as the message of willingness to accommodate, that is, go along with, segregation, at least for the time being.

Northern white reformers and philanthropists soon were asking Washington for advice about which black organizations to support financially. Political leaders turned to him when selecting African Americans to appoint to political positions. With this backing of money and political power, Washington was able to influence the viewpoints of many African-American newspapers, church organizations, and business owners. Wells-Barnett was soon to confront this powerful force.

Meanwhile, laws supporting segregation were spreading throughout the South. There was an active debate raging between various newspapers and special interest groups who focused on the needs and problems of African Americans. It was not unusual for whites openly to speak and write about the "inferiority" or lack of "morality" of Blacks. On the other hand, black leaders were arguing among themselves whether to struggle against or accommodate to the Jim Crow laws.

In the midst of these problems, the U.S. Supreme Court in 1896 announced an extremely important decision in a case dealing with segregation. The case was somewhat like Wells's case against the Chesapeake, Ohio & Southwestern Railroad. In 1890, the state of Louisiana had passed a law requiring all railroad companies carrying passengers in the state to provide "equal but separate accommodations for the white and colored races." The

Louisiana law also required that no person should be permitted to sit in seats in coaches not assigned to his or her race. Homer Plessy, a man who had one great-grandfather who was black, sat in a seat in a passenger car for whites. When ordered to move from that car, he refused to leave his seat. After being forced from the "whites only" car, he had been imprisoned and charged with breaking the law. Plessy lost his case in the Louisiana courts, but he appealed to the United States federal courts. He claimed his rights under the U.S. Constitution had been violated.

By 1896, the case had been appealed all the way to the U.S. Supreme Court, which ruled in an 8-to-1 decision that "separate but equal" facilities for Blacks and whites were acceptable. Plessy's side had argued that segregating them made African Americans wear a "badge of inferiority." Justice Henry B. Brown, who delivered the opinion of the Court, replied that this would be so only "because the colored race chooses to put that construction on it." The *Plessy* v. *Ferguson* decision, which was not

Louisiana train ticket. In its 1896 *Plessy* v. *Ferguson* decision, the U.S. Supreme Court upheld a Louisiana segregation law.

overturned until 1954, opened the way for all kinds of segregation. As a result, whites rushed to set up even more segregated schools, waiting rooms, doctor's offices, theaters, hotels, restaurants, and even rest rooms.

The death of Frederick Douglass and the rise in popularity and influence of Booker T. Washington in 1895 and the "separate but equal" Supreme Court decision in 1896 all had effects on the life of the antilynching crusader. The newly married Ida B. Wells-Barnett was ready to meet the challenges.

Continuing Battles

After her marriage, Ida B. Wells-Barnett continued her activities fighting against lynching and discrimination. She also continued to work to improve the lives of African Americans in Chicago. In responding to the challenges, Wells-Barnett was able to use her skills at getting people to rally around a cause.

The formation of a national organization of African-American women's clubs occurred after a written attack against African-American women. A white editor and president of the Missouri Press Association had sent a letter to one of the leaders of England's Anti-Lynching Society. In it, the editor accused African-American women of being immoral. (Wells-Barnett later claimed that it also attacked her in particular.) The angry English reformer immediately sent a copy of the vicious letter to the president of one of Boston's African-American women's clubs. She, in turn, had copies of the letter sent to African-American women's clubs across the nation and called for a national meeting in Boston. They invited Ida B. Wells-Barnett, but the meeting was to be held right after her wedding. She declined the invitation.

At that July 1895 meeting, the National Federation of Afro-American Women was started. Margaret Murray Washington, whose husband, Booker T. Washington, was calling for accommodation rather than confrontation with whites, was elected the federation's leader. The dispute about which road to travel was heating up. For Wells-Barnett and others, the route to take involved not accommodation but confrontation in the courts and the demand for the rights that are guaranteed in the U.S. Constitution. Wells-Barnett believed that education and economic independence would follow as a result of having people's rights respected.

About nine months after her wedding, Wells-Barnett gave birth to Charles Aked Barnett, the first of her four children. By

Ida B. Wells-Barnett and her son Charles A. Barnett in 1896. In her speeches, she championed voting rights for women.

July 1896, the proud mother and her four-month-old son were on their way to Washington, D.C., for a historic conference. The National Federation of Afro-American Women was meeting with another major group, the National League of Colored Women, to create a single, larger, and more powerful group. Together they could work on women's needs such as the right to vote, as well as deal with specifically African-American issues. Wells-Barnett took an active role in the conference. The two groups united and became the National Association of Colored Women's Clubs. The most powerful African-American women of the day attended the meeting. Among them was Frederick Douglass's only daughter and Harriet Tubman, the brave woman who decades earlier had made many trips into the South to lead slaves to freedom in the North. Margaret Murray Washington, also attended.

After the conference, Wells-Barnett left for a week's visit with her old friend, Helen Douglass, widow of the famous African-American leader. When she returned to Chicago, she was asked by Republican party leaders to speak statewide on the issues of the day. Since Wells-Barnett was nursing her baby, she could only make the long trip if her baby came with her and was cared for while she delivered speeches. So a nurse met her at each Illinois stop and watched her son while she spoke. This was probably one of the first times a woman had continued a speaking tour while traveling with a nursing baby. A major topic of her speeches was the right of women to vote in national elections. That right would require an amendment to the Constitution. Wells-Barnett was determined to see that women had the same voting rights men had.

With a baby of her own, Wells-Barnett realized more than ever the need to develop and train children during their young "plastic" years as she called them. Her experience as a teacher was an advantage because she was aware of a new idea in schooling—kindergartens. These classes for very young children had started in Germany and had only recently appeared in the United States. The Chicago public schools did not at that time provide young children with kindergartens. Wells-Barnett got the Ida B. Wells Club to set up a private kindergarten, which was among the first in Chicago.

Besides providing day care for children so that mothers could work outside the home, the Ida B. Wells Club helped form the first African-American orchestra in Chicago. It also ran a small bank and a job referral service, and it helped orphans and the elderly. It even managed to join the County League of Clubs, becoming the first African-American group to break that segregation barrier. Its motto expressed Wells-Barnett's beliefs: "Helping Hand."

In late 1897, Ferdinand and Ida's second son, Herman K. Barnett, was born. Although Ida apparently hadn't wanted children when she first married, she discovered how her own children opened her eyes to the pleasure of training them well and to the joy of being loved by such precious people. Four years after Herman's birth came their first daughter, who was honored with her mother's name, Ida B. Barnett. Three years later, in 1904, the last child, Alfreda M. Barnett, was born. Ida's children had a kind and loving mother who was strict with them. As they grew older, each child was expected to be responsible for his or her own behavior.

Earlier in 1897, she had decided to slow up her work outside the home and to devote more of her time to her family, which included her husband's two sons from his first marriage. She resigned as president of the Ida B. Wells Club and quit work at the *Conservator*. Over the next few years she would not leave her

Harriet Tubman helped form what became the National Association of Colored Women.

family for long periods of time—yet she continued to be a strong voice when it came to African-American and women's rights.

One of the incidents that caused her to continue her efforts to fight lynching occurred in Lake City, South Carolina. An African American had been appointed postmaster there. A few days later, a mob of several hundred angry whites attacked the new postmaster's house, burning it down and shooting him and his family as they tried to escape the flames. The mob managed to kill the man and one of his children. Because the postmaster had been employed by the federal government, Wells-Barnett, among others, saw this as a time to press for a federal antilynching law. The nation needed a law that outlawed all lynching and that severely punished those in lynch mobs. Wells-Barnett and others turned to the President of the United States, William McKinley, for help. President McKinley had won the election of 1896. In fact, the Barnetts, as loyal members of the Republican party, had supported McKinley during the campaign.

In April 1898, Wells-Barnett, along with her baby, Herman, went to Washington, D.C. There she joined Senator William Mason, seven congressmen from the Chicago area, and several others, in presenting the case to the President:

> Nowhere in the civilized world save [except in] the United States of America do men, possessing all civil and political power, go out in bands of 50 and 5,000 to hunt down, shoot, hang or burn to death a single individual, unarmed and absolutely powerless.
>
> . . . To our appeals for justice the stereotyped reply has been that the government could not interfere in a state matter. Postmaster Baker's case was a federal matter, pure and simple.
>
> . . . We refuse to believe this country, so powerful to defend its citizens abroad, is unable to protect its citizens at home.

While President McKinley was polite and expressed interest in the case, his attention was drawn to something that had happened a few weeks earlier. The American battleship *Maine* had been blown up in the harbor of Cuba's capital city, Havana. By the end of April, the United States declared war on Spain, which owned Cuba. The war kept McKinley from dealing with problems within the United States. McKinley did not push for an antilynching law. Wells-Barnett stayed in Washington a few more weeks trying to convince Congress to help the postmaster's widow financially and to pass an antilynching law. Congress did neither.

In September of 1898, Wells-Barnett traveled to Rochester, New York, where a monument honoring Frederick Douglass was being dedicated. While there, she also helped her old friend T. Thomas Fortune and others form the Afro-American Council. This was designed to be a national organization that would work to achieve full civil rights for all African Americans. Fortune was elected chairman of the executive committee. Wanting those he could trust around him, Fortune got Wells-Barnett elected secretary. The organization planned to meet in a national conference during the next summer, but a bloody race riot in Wilmington, North Carolina, led to another meeting sooner than they had planned.

The problems between Blacks and whites had boiled over into rioting in Wilmington because of controversy over elections and voting rights. Unlike most other Southern states in the late 1890s, North Carolina allowed African Americans to vote. There were even some African Americans who held elective office.

The upcoming 1898 election centered around the question of white rule in the state. White supremacists called for a state constitutional convention that would take away the right of African Americans to vote. The *Wilmington Daily Record*, an African-American-owned newspaper, opposed lynching. During the election campaign, Alex Manly, the editor, wrote that "[e]very Negro lynched is called a 'Big Burley Black Brute' when in fact many of these who have been thus dealt with had white men for their fathers and were not only not 'black and burly' but were sufficiently attractive for white girls of culture . . . to fall in love with them." The reaction from the white press was predictable. White-owned newspapers expressed outrage over the possibility that such an attraction of white women to black men could exist.

The governor of North Carolina stated that "more guns and pistols were sold in the State between 1896 and 1898 than had been sold in the previous twenty years." As the election campaign wore on, white supremacy became a very inflammatory issue.

In Wilmington, the Republican party won control, having received most of the African-American vote. Following that, about 600 whites attacked black neighborhoods and the office of the *Wilmington Daily Record*, burning it to the ground. In the race riot that followed, 10 African Americans were killed and 10 others were placed in jail for rioting. Legally elected officials, both blacks and whites, had fled for their lives. Even the mayor fled to New York. The largest newspaper in North Carolina stated that "Negro rule is at an end in North Carolina forever. The events . . . at Wilmington . . . place that fact beyond question." Wells-Barnett was again among those who felt the need to oppose the taking away of voting rights. Clearly, the time to simply "accommodate" to whites was past.

In November, the Afro-American Council held an emergency conference, partly to protest President McKinley's failure to speak out against the Wilmington riot. Wells-Barnett gave a speech entitled "Mob Violence and Anarchy." In it, she criticized Booker T. Washington's viewpoint that African Americans should achieve economic power before demanding equal political and civil rights. She also lashed out against the President's failure to act against the rioters in Wilmington. At the conference she was elected the Afro-American Council's financial secretary. That happened despite opposition to Wells-Barnett from those who wanted a man to hold that important position, and preferably a man who agreed with Booker T. Washington's ideas.

Wells-Barnett continued to be active in Chicago as well as on the national scene. By the late 1890s, there were six African-American women's clubs in Chicago; the Ida B. Wells Club had been the first of them. When plans were made by the National Association of Colored Women to hold their convention in Chicago in 1899, Wells-Barnett, among others, saw the need for

Mary Church Terrell, president of the National Association of Colored Women.

the local clubs to combine temporarily. When they did, Wells-Barnett expected to speak to the combined Chicago group—and later probably be elected president of the whole National Association of Colored Women. But she was not even invited to the meetings of the combined local groups or to the national convention. When she asked why, an old acquaintance from Memphis, Mary Church Terrell, told her that members of the other clubs had threatened to withdraw if she spoke at the meetings. Whether that was the truth or not, it was even more painful for Wells-Barnett when Terrell was elected president.

Apparently, Ida B. Wells's personality and determination were good for leading a crusade but not for working with society women in political and civic clubs. She may also have been rejected because she didn't have much of a sense of humor. This lack probably came from years of single-mindedly leading her own crusade. No doubt, the many supporters of Booker T. Washington also had something to do with the situation. After all, one of the guest speakers was Booker T. Washington himself.

One person who had invited Ida B. Wells-Barnett to attend meetings was Jane Addams, one of the country's leading reformers and social workers. Addams, who was a few years older than Wells-Barnett, came from a wealthy white family and was college educated. She had a deep concern for the poor and had started Hull House as a settlement house in a Chicago slum in 1889. She led causes for the poor, demanding child labor laws to protect children from working too many hours, and she fought for improved schools, parks, and housing. Her work centered on immigrants regardless of race.

Addams was like Wells-Barnett in her total dedication, in her use of the press to tell her story, and in her belief in the rights of women. With the two of them struggling for many of the same things in the same city, they naturally became good friends. Wells-Barnett once said that Addams was "the greatest woman in the United States." She was happy to be invited to lunch at Hull House while the combined Chicago women's clubs were planning to hold the national association meetings without her.

When the National Association of Colored Women finally met in Chicago that August, Ida B. Wells-Barnett was busy at another meeting in the city. It happened that the Afro-American Council was also holding its national conference in Chicago during the same month. Wells-Barnett was honored to be reelected as its financial secretary. Instead, she asked to be put in charge of the organization's Anti-Lynching Bureau. In that position, she would be able to continue her work of collecting information about lynchings from all over the country.

By 1899, the division in the Afro-American Council between the supporters and opponents of Booker T. Washington was even sharper than during its

Jane Addams. She and Ida B. Wells-Barnett became good friends.

1898 meetings. One of the young leaders who opposed Washington's position was W. E. B. Du Bois, at that time a professor at Atlanta University. W. E. B. Du Bois, born in 1868 in Massachusetts, had attended Fisk University in Tennessee and had received a Ph.D. from Harvard University. Like Wells-Barnett, he had agreed with some of Booker T. Washington's ideas such as the importance of work, thrift, and African-American unity. But soon Du Bois came to believe that Jim Crow laws, lynchings, and discrimination were not going to end just because African Americans might gain economic security. African Americans needed to protest against segregation and to demand their political and civil rights. He thought that a small group of college-educated African Americans (whom he later called "the talented tenth") could help lead a movement to achieve full freedom.

Over the next few years, the Afro-American Council was divided between supporters of Washington, including Wells-Barnett's old friend T. Thomas Fortune, and supporters of a more militant position, including people like Wells-Barnett and Du Bois. By the time Fortune was elected its president in 1902, the organization had lost most of its effectiveness in the fight against lynching and segregation.

During those years, the number of lynchings declined, but it remained a very serious problem and other violence against African Americans continued. One of the most serious disturbances occurred in New Orleans, Louisiana, in 1900. Only four years earlier, the Supreme Court had upheld a Louisiana segregation law in the famous *Plessy* v. *Ferguson* decision. During a warm July in New Orleans, two African-American men were sitting outside their homes. They were approached by three police officers who tried to arrest them on a charge of burglary. A fight broke out. One of the African Americans was wounded and two of the policemen were killed. Somehow, one of the African Americans, Robert Charles, escaped. A $250 reward for Charles's capture, dead or alive, was offered. In the manhunt, two more officers were killed by Robert Charles, who was still at large.

As the African-American section of New Orleans was searched, roaming white gangs attacked innocent black men. The following day, the city was in the hands of a white mob. Black women were beaten, and black hospitals were attacked. Charles was finally cornered and shot to death while fighting for his life. For several days the city was gripped by fear, hatred, and riots.

After things calmed down, Wells-Barnett began a thorough investigation of the riot and what kind of a "monster" Robert Charles was accused of being. His room was filled with religious works, and he apparently had been on a religious mission. He did not appear to be the murderous criminal that events had made him appear.

In response to the information she gathered about the violence, Wells-Barnett wrote a 48-page pamphlet entitled *Mob Rule in New Orleans*, explaining what really happened. Once again, Ida B. Wells-Barnett had used the pen to lash out at those who lynched African Americans out of senseless hatred. Once again she urged an end to lynching, violence, and discrimination against African Americans.

CHAPTER NINE

Disappointment and Determination

Following the bloody New Orleans riot of 1900, many militant African Americans started working together to try once and for all to end segregation and white violence against Blacks. Although Ida B. Wells-Barnett continued to deal with national issues, her main focus was on Chicago.

One of the new young leaders was Dr. W. E. B. Du Bois, the intellectual college professional Wells-Barnett had met earlier. He strongly believed that black Africans and people descended from them throughout the world had common interests. They should work together to improve their conditions. In 1900, he had been one of the leaders of the first Pan-African Conference held in London, England. That meeting demanded better treatment of Africans by their European colonial rulers. Du Bois's most important book, *The Souls of Black Folk*, was published in 1903. In it, he attacked the accommodationist views of Booker T. Washington, as had Ida B. Wells-Barnett several years earlier.

In 1904, Du Bois brought together several of the strongest writers in the African-American community to speak with one voice against the accommodating methods

W. E. B. Du Bois. He opposed Booker T. Washington's policies.

of Booker T. Washington. Entitled *The Negro Problem from the Negro Point of View*, the published collection of essays was a direct call to stop following Booker T. Washington.

Du Bois's book included a powerful article, "Booker T. Washington and His Critics," by Wells-Barnett, first printed in the *World Today*. In it, she attacked Washington's stand on education for African Americans:

> Industrial [vocational] education for the Negro is Booker T. Washington's hobby. He believes that for the masses of the Negro race an elementary education of the brain and a continuation of the education of the hand is not only the best kind, but . . . is the most popular with the white South.

She was referring to the policy of keeping African Americans working as unskilled or skilled laborers rather than as well-educated professionals and business people. As a former teacher, she did not believe that accommodation was in the best interests of African Americans. Wells-Barnett praised the Freedmen's Aid Society, the American Missionary Association, and others who had helped people like her to use their minds to improve themselves and other African Americans. She pointed out the importance of schools and teaching for all African Americans:

> They have given us thousands of teachers for our schools in the South, physicians to heal our ailments, druggists, lawyers and ministers. . . . They have given us 2,000 college graduates, over half of whom own property worth over $1,000 per capita. [At that time $1,000 per person was quite a bit—the average worker earned only about $432 a year.] The Negro owes a debt of gratitude which he can never repay to the hundreds of self-sacrificing teachers who gave their lives to the work of Negro education.

Her anger rose as she stated what the effect of Booker T. Washington's teachings was:

> The result is that the world which listens to him and which largely supports his educational institution [Tuskegee Institute], has almost unanimously decided that college education is a mistake for the Negro.

Wells-Barnett objected to the fact that money went to only a few African-American schools such as the Tuskegee Institute. She believed that African Americans needed many academic schools and colleges for a wide variety of types of education. Booker T. Washington was, instead, influencing wealthy reformers to give their money to only his type of limited schooling. She claimed that the results of Washington's policies were lost opportunities for African Americans, whom she called "black diamonds buried in the . . . black South."

Wells-Barnett then turned to the horrors of lynching. She again criticized Washington's belief that when African Americans became more educated they would stop committing crimes and so lynching would stop. Wells-Barnett insisted that lynchings were not the revenge for real crimes committed but the result of white bigotry based on racial hatred. In striking out so boldly at Booker T. Washington, Wells-Barnett was directly breaking with one of the most popular and respected African Americans of the day. She felt he simply did not understand the problems of African Americans as well as she did. Such bold actions enraged many African Americans, which may help explain why she was not more loved for her crusades.

When it came to solving problems, Wells-Barnett saw there was plenty to do right in Chicago. The African-American population there had grown tremendously because of the migration of people from the rural South. Most African Americans lived in the southwestern part of the city. Although they were not totally segregated, there were increasing numbers of African-American churches, clubs, and neighborhoods. They often competed for jobs and housing with the growing population of poor European immigrants who had come to the United States seeking a better way of life. Wells-Barnett opposed segregation and wanted to keep Blacks and whites working and living together in the same neighborhoods. For example, when one of the powerful white-owned newspapers in Chicago began a campaign to segregate the public schools, she fought back. With her friend Jane Addams and others, she held meetings that put pressure on the newspaper to stop pushing for segregated city schools.

At this time, Wells-Barnett began working with Celia Parker Wooley, one of the city's leading white reformers. Wooley had founded the Frederick Douglass Center, a settlement house in a neighborhood near both Blacks and whites. Wells-Barnett apparently expected to be elected president of the women's club that ran many of the settlement house's activities. But a white woman was elected president instead, and Wells-Barnett, unhappily, became vice president. She was even more displeased when the club focused on harmony among middle-class Blacks and whites in the neighborhood and on athletics rather than solving the problems of the poor in the area.

Although the group was successful, Wells-Barnett didn't like it. Once again, she suffered the disappointment of not being elected to the top position despite her work. Once again, she had refused to modify her goals in order to achieve power in an organization. She was not about to worry about whom she offended once on a crusade. That did not endear her to those who got in her way.

In 1905, there was important progress made against lynching in Illinois, largely as a result of Wells-Barnett's work. The only African-American state legislator in Illinois, with the help of Governor Charles S. Deneen, had been able to get a state anti-lynching law passed. The 1905 Mob Violence Act also made it illegal for a sheriff in Illinois to turn over a prisoner to a lynch mob. The effectiveness of the law would soon be tested.

Meanwhile the Afro-American Council had not lived up to its ambitious beginnings and no longer welcomed the ideas of militant civil rights activists. These activists began to plan for another way to achieve their goals. Led by Du Bois, a small group that included Wells-Barnett held a meeting in July 1905 near Niagara Falls in the village of Fort Erie, Ontario, Canada. They met in Canada because they had run into discrimination at a hotel on the New York State side of the Canadian–U.S. border.

Soon known as the Niagara Movement, this protest group laid the blame for black problems squarely on white America. The founders of the Niagara Movement opposed *all* segregation, *all* laws designed to deprive African Americans of their right to vote, and *all* mob violence against African Americans. Du Bois, Wells-Barnett, and other founders of the Niagara Movement demanded liberal education, which went far beyond the vocational education called for by Booker T. Washington. They were against all compromise with white racists.

Booker T. Washington and his followers worked hard to discredit this radical movement by paying or pressuring much of the African-American-owned press to either ignore or oppose the activities of the Niagara Movement. Unable to get strong financial backing and troubled by disagreements among its leaders, the Niagara Movement struggled on. Meanwhile, Wells-Barnett was devoting her time and energy to her family and to Chicago's problems. As a result, she was not very active in the Niagara Movement. Without broad black and white support, it slowly weakened until it ended in 1910.

In the South, and increasingly in the North, the old problem of white violence against African Americans continued. Major riots occurred in Atlanta, Georgia, in 1906, and in Springfield, Illinois, in 1908. The Springfield riot was particularly violent. The city of Springfield, the Illinois state capital, had a population of about 60,000, of whom 4,500 were African Americans. Many of the Blacks had recently arrived from the South and were competing with whites for jobs. A major problem occurred when a nearby mine hired African Americans as strikebreakers.

The riot started after a white woman accused a black man of rape. The man charged with the rape had been jailed, and when the mob couldn't get to him, it lynched two other black men, instead. One of them was 84 years old and had been married to a white woman for 30 years. In two days of violence, much of the city was damaged by fires the mob started. The riot destroyed property worth $120,000, and 4,000 Illinois state militia troops were needed to restore order, at an additional cost of $200,000. Later, the white woman who claimed she had been raped admitted that she had made up the charge. All this happened in the city where Abraham Lincoln, signer of the Emancipation Proclamation, had lived and been buried.

Among those who protested the Springfield race riot were leading white and black writers, religious leaders, and reformers. They turned to Oswald Garrison Villard, grandson of William Lloyd Garrison, the famous white journalist who had opposed slavery. Like his grandfather, Villard was stirred into action. Fifty-three of the nation's best-known and most respected African Americans, including Ida B. Wells-Barnett and W. E. B. Du Bois, signed a statement issued by Villard. This "Call" urged that a meeting be held by all concerned about justice and full civil and political rights for African Americans. It was time to unite!

The meeting was scheduled for May 31 through June 1, 1909. One thousand invitations were sent out nationally, including one to Booker T. Washington, who did not attend. A major event was expected at this meeting, which was called the National Negro Conference.

Because the National Negro Conference had a great many white members, there was concern about who would control the organization being formed. Wells-Barnett was recognized as someone who needed to be heard by the assembly. She had been honored to be among the 25 people asked to speak to this important group. In a stirring and powerful address entitled "Lynching: Our National Crime," she lashed out at lynching as "color line murder," which was a "national crime" that needed "a national remedy." The call for a national law against lynch mobs was again forcefully repeated.

In her speech, later printed in the proceedings of the National Negro Conference, Ida B. Wells-Barnett noted that the "lynching record for a quarter of a century merits the thoughtful study of the American people. It presents three . . . facts: First: Lynching is color line murder. Second: Crimes against women is the excuse, not the cause. Third: It is a national crime and requires a national remedy." She continued: "From 1882, in which year 52 were lynched, down to the present, lynching has been along the color line. Mob murder increased yearly until in 1892 more than 200 victims were lynched. . . . 3,284 men, women and children have been put to death in this quarter of a century."

Wells-Barnett with Charles, Herman, Ida, and Alfreda in 1909. That year she wrote "Lynching: Our National Crime."

She went on to explain that from 1899 to 1908, a total of 959 people had been lynched, with 857 of them being African American. Of that number, 28 were burned at the stake, including a woman and two children! She cried out, "Why is the mob murder permitted by a Christian nation?" But she wasn't done; she broke down statistics of the 285 lynchings for which a "cause" could be found. The "excuses" included such things as "no cause, 10," "bad reputation, 8," "unpopularity, 3," "insulting language to a woman, 5," and "throwing stones, 1." She concluded: "The only perfect remedy is an appeal to law." It was powerful information, all the more because lynching had once been mostly a Southern problem, but was now national in scope.

Since millions of African Americans would be represented by the organization, a one-year study by a Committee of Forty was proposed. The Committee of Forty would set up the new organization. Only 12 African Americans were named to the committee! Although accommodationists were not included—Booker T. Washington's name was not on the list—most of the African Americans were moderates. Du Bois was the only member of the more militant Niagara Movement on the committee. Wells-Barnett found out that Du Bois himself had removed her name from the list of 40 members and had replaced her with another Niagara Movement member who was not even present at the time. But other militant African Americans were also excluded. Her radical viewpoints probably cost her acceptance by moderate white and black leaders. Nevertheless, at the urging of some of the white leaders, Wells-Barnett was finally made a member of the committee.

The Committee of Forty had major work to do. It explained it represented "10,000,000 colored fellow citizens" who were often denied "their just share of the public funds, robbed of nearly all part in government, segregated by common carriers [public transportation], some murdered . . . , and all treated with open contempt . . . [while] held in some States in practical slavery by the white community."

Meanwhile, the senseless violence continued. In Cairo, Illinois, a white woman was found murdered on November 11, 1909. Once again the police looked for an African American to blame for the murder. They found William "Frog" James, whom Wells-Barnett later described as a "shiftless, penniless colored man" who "could not give a good account of himself." He was charged with rape and murder and locked up.

A crowd grew around the jail, so County Sheriff Frank Davis and one deputy took James to another town for the night. When they were discovered and forced to return to Cairo the next day, the now-huge mob attacked James, put a rope around his neck, and hanged him from a light pole. Not satisfied, the lynch mob then started shooting at the lifeless body, hitting it over 500 times! When a bullet cut the rope, the lifeless body fell to the ground. Still not satisfied, the mob used a carriage to drag the body around the town with the mob in pursuit. Finally, stopping near where the dead white woman had been found, the head was ripped off and stuck on a fence post, and the body was burned. No one seemed concerned that the poor man might have been innocent!

So crazy with bloodthirst was the mob that someone yelled: "Let's get Salzner!" Salzner was a white man under arrest in the same jail for murdering his wife. When the mob reached the jailhouse, Sheriff Davis begged them to go away. Banging against the doors, the mob would not stop. This time the sheriff called the governor's office for help. But the crowd broke in, grabbed Henry Salzner, and hanged him, spending the last of their bullets in his lifeless body. By the time help arrived, the mob had gone home.

A few years earlier, Illinois had passed a law providing that a sheriff who handed over a prisoner to a mob could be dismissed from his job. Governor Charles S. Deneen suspended the sheriff. However, that same law allowed a dismissed sheriff to ask for his job back. Davis planned to do just that. Ferdinand L. Barnett, who was the assistant state attorney, tried to get some of Chicago's African-American leaders to go to the state capital to argue against the sheriff's getting his job back. When they refused to help out and it appeared no charges would be filed following the lynchings, Ferdinand and Ida discussed the situation. Ferdinand urged Ida to go to Cairo to gather information and then present the facts to Governor Deneen in Springfield. Looking at her baby, Ida wanted to stay home with her young children, but her husband insisted. For once she wasn't sure. But her oldest son, Charles, now 13, said it all: "Mother if you don't go nobody else will." She left the next morning.

Wells-Barnett's investigation was thorough, as usual. With the help of an African-American lawyer in Cairo, the Barnetts then prepared an explanation of the riot for the governor. The sheriff had not fulfilled his proper duties. Sheriff Davis had claimed that the mob knocked him aside and that there was nothing that could be done to stop them. But after an exhaustive review, Governor Deneen forcefully upheld the Barnetts' findings. Frank Davis did not get back his job as sheriff. Deneen stated, "Mob law has no place in Illinois." Lynching would finally be ended in Illinois.

Meanwhile, the Committee of Forty had been planning to meet in New York in May 1910. Wells-Barnett had been invited, but she wrote that she could not afford the cost of attending. The offer was made to pay all her expenses, so she felt she had to go. At the meeting, W. E. B. Du Bois was placed in charge of publicity and research. The group also decided on a name: the National Association for the Advancement of Colored People, or NAACP as it is widely known today. The NAACP pledged to work for an end to segregation and discrimination in education, transportation, jobs, and housing. It would also investigate lynching, injustice in the courts, and lack of voting rights.

Wells-Barnett still resented Du Bois's 1909 attempt to exclude her from the Committee of Forty. She also did not like Villard's and Du Bois's ideas about keeping control of the NAACP in the hands of a small group of college-educated leaders. Du Bois did not even want to mention Wells-Barnett in the pages of the *Crisis*, the NAACP's official publication. Insulted, instead of becoming an active leader in the NAACP, Wells-Barnett devoted herself to other activities in Chicago.

Wells-Barnett wanted to meet the needs of African Americans in Chicago, particularly the poor and the thousands of people migrating from the South to the North. Following the 1908 Springfield race riot, she became involved in forming a group to solve some of the problems. After investigating riots and lynchings, including one in Joliet, Illinois, she concluded that free, idle time for African-American males of school age could lead to trouble. She concluded that there were not enough organized activities for them. She found, for example, that the local YMCAs in Chicago did not meet the needs of African Americans. Wells-Barnett discussed the situation with some of the young African Americans she taught in a Sunday Bible class. They organized into a group called the Negro Fellowship League.

The Negro Fellowship League decided to establish a settlement house for troubled African-American youth who lived in southeastern Chicago. With the financial help of Mrs. Victor Lawson, whose husband was the editor of the Chicago *Daily News*, a settlement house was opened on State Street in May 1910. Wells-Barnett chose the name for the settlement house—the Light House—because she wanted it to be like a lighthouse, a place that would give direction and guidance.

The Light House had a reading room and a job placement service to help young African Americans find productive jobs. The office was soon busy with 40 or 50 people coming in daily. Sometimes young men were even put up for the night. Wells-Barnett worked without pay, although the secretary was paid $75 a month. They used the building for three years thanks to the support of the Lawsons. Wells-Barnett continued as the president of the Negro Fellowship League and organized Light House activities such as lectures and concerts.

Wells-Barnett must have looked back at the first dozen or so years of the century with pride, disappointment, and determination. Her cause was known worldwide, and she had made some definite progress in her personal war against lynching. Her militant positions and assertiveness were also offensive to some, so she was not being asked to serve on national committees. But Ida B. Wells-Barnett had a strong family and a husband who was also successful and who fully supported her activities. She knew that she had already accomplished much, and she wasn't done yet!

CHAPTER TEN

Final Gifts

Ida B. Wells-Barnett turned 48 in 1910. She continued working to solve problems in Chicago where she concentrated her efforts. She had been so successful at finding young people jobs that some private job services complained that the Light House didn't have an employment agency license! In order to continue her volunteer work, she had to pay the state $50 a year for the license.

Even with the responsibilities of her family and the full-time volunteer job at the Light House, Wells-Barnett continued to make time to write. In 1910, she wrote an article about enfranchisement, the gaining of the right to vote. "How Enfranchisement Stops Lynching" was published in *Original Rights Magazine*. She stated her firm belief that, given the right to vote, African Americans could help elect a government that would make sure they gained their full rights as citizens. One of the main effects of Jim Crow laws in the South was to deny African Americans the right to vote—a right guaranteed to African Americans by the 15th Amendment to the U.S. Constitution. In addition, women in many states were still not allowed to vote in national elections and in most state and local elections as well. There was a need to provide and enforce voting rights for the majority of American adults who were still denied those rights.

In the article, Wells-Barnett reviewed the history of African-American citizenship. She started with the "flower of nineteenth century civilization" meaning the end of slavery and the enfranchisement of all men in the United States. She briefly described how white violence and voter fraud stole from the African American "his only protection to his citizenship—his vote." She noted how the government had kept itself busy "repealing the civil rights bill, affirming Jim Crow legislation, . . . and removing in every way possible the constitutional guarantees to life, liberty and the pursuit of happiness . . . and the Negro must now look out for himself."

She bitterly noted the following:

> He [the African American] was advised that if he gave up trying to vote, minded his own business, acquired property and educated his children, he could get along in the South without molestation. But the more lands and houses he acquired, the more rapidly discriminating laws have been passed against him by those who control the ballot, and [the] less protection is given by the lawmakers for his life, liberty and property. The Negro has been given separate and inferior schools, because he has no ballot. He therefore cannot protest against such legislation by choosing other law makers, or retiring to private life those who legislate against his interests. The more he sends his children to school the more restrictions are placed on Negro education, and he has absolutely no voice in the disposition [use] of the school funds his taxes help to supply. . . .
>
> With no sacredness of the ballot there can be no sacredness of human life itself. For if the strong can take the weak man's ballot, when it suits his purpose to do so, he will take his life also. . . . . [T]he more complete the disenfranchisement, the more frequent and horrible has been the hangings, shootings, and burnings."

Wells-Barnett then told the stories of the Springfield riot and Cairo lynchings. She pointed out that after Governor Deneen's firing of Sheriff Davis, three times in two years other sheriffs had managed to stop mobs from lynching someone. In 1910, for example, some of the people of Cairo had formed a mob enraged over the stealing of a purse. Learning that a mob was being formed, the new sheriff brought in men to defend the jail where the two men charged with the crime were being held. When the mob arrived, the sheriff warned them not to enter. The leader pushed on, shots rang out from inside the jail, and the leader of the mob fell dead, with others wounded around him. The dead man was the son of a former mayor of Cairo. Leaders of the mob were arrested and awaiting trial at the time Wells-Barnett wrote the article. It seemed that progress was being made.

From 1910 to 1913, Wells-Barnett worked as a volunteer every day at the Light House and with the Negro Fellowship League. In 1911, the league started a newspaper called the *Fellowship Herald*, which she edited. It did not do well. The old problems of not getting along with others and having people question her intentions reappeared. Then Mrs. Lawson died, leaving the sponsorship of the Light House unclear.

For a while, Victor Lawson continued to provide money for Wells-Barnett's settlement house. But when a YMCA building designed to serve the needs of the African-American community was opened, community leaders urged Lawson to support it rather than the Light House. He withdrew his support for the Light House, pointing out that nearly $9,000 had been given by Mrs. Lawson in support of the Negro Fellowship League. He felt that others should now be as generous.

Rather than close the settlement house, the Negro Fellowship League moved the Light House to a storefront; the rent was much lower—only $35 a month instead of $175. It was small and crowded, but Ida B. Wells-Barnett wasn't about to give up.

In 1913, with determination, Wells-Barnett decided to start a new career at the age of 50. A local judge had asked her if she would work as an adult probation officer. Probation officers investigate, report on, and supervise the conduct of convicted criminals who rather than being in prison are under supervision as part of their sentence. As a probation officer, Wells-Barnett helped her clients adjust to life outside prison and maintain good behavior.

Wells-Barnett was the first adult probation officer in Chicago history who was an African-American woman. She started working in the city courthouse but soon moved her office to the Light House. There she could really help the people who reported to her. Her salary of $150 a month helped keep the Light House's projects going. (She held the probation officer's job until 1916.)

Also in 1913, Wells-Barnett took up another cause, helping organize the Alpha Suffrage Club. That group was dedicated to getting the right to vote for women in general and for African-American women in particular. The Alpha Suffrage Club, with Wells-Barnett as its president, held weekly meetings at the Negro Fellowship League office. As she had always done, Wells-Barnett linked her various causes together; she even met with female prisoners to educate them about the importance of voting. One of the biggest concerns of the club was whether or not women would vote in national elections if given the chance.

The Alpha Suffrage Club sent her to Washington, D.C. There she was supposed to join other well-known women demonstrating in front of the White House. It was the day before Woodrow Wilson would take office as President of the United States in 1913. Some of the Southern white women's rights leaders did not want whites and Blacks to be seen marching together. But Wells-Barnett marched at the front of the demonstration, in a rare position of honor, instead of in a separate African-American part of the march. She got there by cutting in just as the demonstration started and it was too late to remove her!

Later that same year, women gained the right to vote on some issues (but not all) in the state of Illinois. The Alpha Suffrage Club worked hard to convince African-American women in Chicago to register and vote in those elections. But women were still not allowed to vote for candidates for national office like that of President of the United States.

By 1915, the African-American population of Chicago had reached 50,000 as more people continued to move from the South to the North. When World War I had begun in Europe in 1914, the number of immigrants entering the United States declined. However, the problems between African Americans and immigrants continued. Many of the problems arose because of conflicts about jobs. Historically, owners and managers of factories denied African Americans jobs in factories. The only time they seemed to be hired was when the factory owners wanted them to break strikes. This was yet another way poor Blacks and poor whites were divided against each other while their wages were kept down.

Most labor unions excluded African Americans from membership or kept them segregated within the labor movement. To add to the conflicts between different racial and ethnic groups, there was a housing shortage. Many whites refused to sell houses to Blacks or new immigrants. That only made the competition for limited housing worse.

A few years earlier, in 1910, what later came to be called the National Urban League had been organized. Its goals were to help African Americans from the rural South find work and housing in the Northern cities. It also tried to improve their education and living conditions and help them adjust to city life. In 1915, the Chicago branch of the Urban League was organized. It began to take financial support away from groups like the Negro Fellowship League. Wells-Barnett once again found herself resented by other African-American leaders. Her efforts to keep the Negro Fellowship League strong were seen as attempts to prevent the Chicago Urban League from growing.

By 1916, the size and influence of the Negro Fellowship League had declined. The year after that, the Chicago political leaders Wells-Barnett supported lost an election. As a result she lost her job as a probation officer when the new politicians came into office. Since she no longer had the probation officer salary to help out the Negro Fellowship League, it was in even more trouble financially.

In April 1917, the United States entered World War I. Many industries switched to producing wartime supplies and weapons. The African-American migration from the South increased rapidly as new jobs were created by the war. Between 1910 and 1920, the number of African Americans in Chicago almost doubled to 100,000. Many of the men who moved to the North found work in heavy industries such as steel and auto making, shipbuilding, mining, and meatpacking. In some cases, factory owners were desperate for workers because of the labor shortage caused by the military draft. Although many unions resisted having African-American members, some, like the meatpacking workers in Chicago, welcomed them. But even in the heavy industries, they usually got the worst, lowest-paying jobs. And about half of all African-American women employed in the North worked as household workers and servants.

East St. Louis, Illinois, was one of the cities undergoing major economic and social change. Many African Americans either passed through or settled in the rail and river crossroads of East St. Louis. The owners and managers of factories in the poor industrial area were looking for cheap labor. African Americans from rural areas were willing to work for low wages rather than not have a job at all. But workers in the whites-only unions saw their jobs being taken by needy Blacks. White workers attacked Blacks in May 1917. The stage was set for more trouble because the city government did little about the attack.

There were minor problems almost weekly after that. But on July 1, some whites drove through black neighborhoods shooting

East St. Louis race riot of 1917. A white mob is about to attack an African American, who is in front of the trolley car.

into the houses. This time, however, the Blacks shot back. Sent to investigate, the police arrived in automobiles similar to the white workers' cars, so the Blacks shot at them as well. Two officers died in the shooting. The next day, full-scale battles broke out. White mobs set fire to the houses of Blacks, burning the people alive or gunning them down if they tried to escape from the flames.

Police and state militia did little or nothing to stop the violence. Some even helped the white mobs. In the race riot, 39 Blacks and 8 whites died. Many African Americans fled to the safety of St. Louis, across the Mississippi River. Fires destroyed $370,000 worth of property; 244 buildings were burned down.

In response to these riots, the Negro Fellowship League met, and it decided that Ida B. Wells-Barnett should go to East St. Louis to investigate the situation and then make a report to the

In 1917, the NAACP held a Silent Protest Parade in New York City to protest the race riots and lynchings.

Illinois governor. She left Chicago the next day. Right after the riot, East St. Louis was a dangerous place for any African American to enter. But that didn't stop Wells-Barnett. She walked alone on streets with burned-out buildings where few people were seen. She managed to interview survivors and gather information.

When she returned home, she found out that a more moderate African-American group from Chicago had already met with the governor, telling him not to pay attention to what the Negro Fellowship League said. Nevertheless, she went to Springfield, the state capital, and presented her report to the governor. Meanwhile, Congress sent a committee to investigate the problem. It seemed to place much of the blame on local authorities in East St. Louis. But when Wells-Barnett went back to East St. Louis, she found that whites were trying to place the blame for the riots on Blacks.

Wells-Barnett used an African-American newspaper, the *Chicago Defender*, to publicize her findings. The power of the press once more made the truth known. Innocent African Americans who were wrongly blamed for what happened in East St. Louis were freed from jail as a direct result.

By the end of 1918, the United States and its Allies had won World War I. The troops began coming home in huge numbers. The men had been changed by the war—most had never traveled abroad before or even met people from all parts of their country. During the war, women had held jobs men had filled before. Businesses were in the midst of changing from making war supplies and weapons to the items people bought in peacetime. African-American men who had served patriotically (although in segregated military units) returned home, expecting to have rights as veterans. They certainly expected to find jobs waiting for them. These veterans soon discovered that while they were good enough to die for their country, finding work in it was another matter. The old conflicts between whites and Blacks began to reappear, especially over jobs, housing, education, and recreational facilities.

In 1918, the Barnett family moved to a large house in a mainly white neighborhood in Chicago. Many of the whites did not welcome Blacks. By mid-1919, several nearby homes of Blacks and of whites who rented or sold homes to them were bombed. The situation in Chicago was growing more tense.

It was a time of great unrest not just in Chicago, but also across the United States. Many people were having a hard time adjusting to the peacetime economy. During 1919, more than 4 million workers went on strike for higher pay and better working conditions.

The bombings of neighboring homes and attacks on African-American children led Wells-Barnett to once again take action. She wrote a letter to the editor of Chicago's biggest newspaper, the *Chicago Tribune*. Her letter was published on July 7. In it she attacked white community leaders and city officials in Chicago for the worsening racial conflicts in the city. She asked if Chicago

Wells-Barnett (shown here in 1917 with her husband and their children and grandchildren) continued her antilynching crusade.

was trying to rival the South in its race hatred against African Americans. She compared the situation to that of East St. Louis in the weeks before that city had been torn by riots. She wrote that officials should take action against lawbreakers before it was too late. Her warnings were ignored.

Twenty days later, fighting broke out at a Chicago beach used by whites and Blacks. It began after a young black swimmer was discovered in a part of the water whites were using. A stone was thrown and killed the swimmer. The riot spread as white mobs attacked black neighborhoods. Many of the African Americans were war veterans and decided to defend themselves and fight back. The battles lasted for five days. Fifteen whites and 23 Blacks were killed, hundreds were injured, and many buildings burned and destroyed. The state militia had to be called in to restore order. A state government committee investigated the riots and came up with conclusions similar to Wells-Barnett's.

The next year, 1920, saw both victory and defeat for Ida B. Wells-Barnett. The 19th Amendment to the Constitution was approved. Women across the United States had finally gained the

A white mob stands next to the burning body of an African American brutally lynched in 1919.

right to vote. But that same year she had to watch as the Light House closed its doors on State Street. Its job was not done, but it had run out of funds. Wells-Barnett had offered much of her rich life to making the settlement house as successful as possible. Within a few weeks, she had to undergo gallbladder surgery from which she made a slow recovery.

A tragic incident soon caught Wells-Barnett's interest. Near the Arkansas town of Elaine in rural Phillips County, many people had been killed in race riots. The problem had begun when African-American tenant farmers and sharecroppers had been forced to sell their cotton below the market price. In 1919, they decided to form a union. They refused to sell their cotton at such a low price to the white cotton buyers. The white reaction was quick. Angry armed whites, not only from Arkansas but also from nearby Tennessee and Mississippi, poured into Phillips County. They attacked and killed black farmers, who tried to defend themselves as best they could. Approximately 5 whites and between 20 and 120 Blacks were killed in the fighting.

Hundreds of black men and women were arrested. Many of them were charged with murder and with planning to kill whites and take over their land. The Arkansas trial lasted less than an hour, and the all-white jury took six minutes to find the accused guilty. Many African Americans were sentenced to prison terms, and 12 of them were sentenced to death in the electric chair.

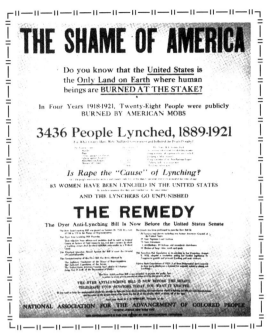

A 1922 newspaper ad favoring a proposed federal antilynching bill.

When Wells-Barnett learned about the incident and the unfair trial, she wrote a letter to the *Chicago Defender*. Soon people held protest meetings. They collected money for the legal defense of the condemned men. They sent letters and telegrams to the Arkansas governor. New trials were scheduled. But when an NAACP investigator tried to interview the prisoners, he was almost lynched and was forced to leave town. Fortunately, the jailed men had sent a letter to the *Chicago Defender*, thanking it for its help, and the letter had included an address. Wells-Barnett learned that the Little Rock, Arkansas, address was that of the mother of one of the condemned men. Despite the great danger, 59-year-old Ida B. Wells-Barnett decided that she would go to Arkansas to investigate the situation herself.

In early 1922, Wells-Barnett traveled to the South for the first time in many years. With the help of the address from the letter sent to the *Chicago Defender*, she was able to meet personally with family members of the condemned men. Then, dressed like the condemned men's mothers and wives, she was able to go with them when they visited the prisoners. Fortunately, the guard did not recognize her. In this way, Wells-Barnett was able quietly to gather information about the riots and killings from the prisoners. Later, the jailed men and their wives and mothers began singing spirituals as well as songs they had composed. Wells-Barnett told them: "You have sung and prayed about dying and forgiving your enemies. . . . Why don't you pray to live and ask to be freed? . . .Quit talking about dying. Pray to live and believe you are going to get out."

After Wells-Barnett had collected information from the prisoners, their lawyer, their families, and the local black community, she returned to Chicago. She wrote a pamphlet entitled *The Arkansas Race Riot*, publicizing the facts about the case. Many people learned for the first time about the great injustice that had been done. Finally, in 1923, the court ruled that the trial had not been a fair one. All the prisoners were eventually freed.

In 1924, Ida B. Wells-Barnett ran for the presidency of the National Association of Colored Women. The old problems of her assertive behavior again appeared, and she was not elected. That did not stop her from being active. She continued to give lectures, attend meetings, and write, although most of her time was spent in Chicago with her children and grandchildren.

Ida B. Wells-Barnett also continued her political activity. She and her husband had long been active in city and state politics as members of the Republican party. Barnett had served as assistant state's attorney from 1896 to 1911. Wells-Barnett had for decades participated in Republican women's organizations. With the 1928 presidential election coming, and with women having the vote, she helped the presidential candidate of the Republican party, Herbert Hoover. Before the election, Wells-Barnett worked in 10 Illinois counties getting African-American women to register to vote. Many more African-American women voted in Illinois than ever before.

By 1930, Chicago was second only to New York City in the population of African Americans. Wells-Barnett had devoted nearly 40 years to the growth and welfare of her adopted city. She obviously felt that it was time for an African-American woman to run for state office. So, at the age of 68, she decided to run for the Illinois State Senate. Wells-Barnett wrote thousands of cards and

In 1927, prominent Chicagoans met to honor Ida B. Wells-Barnett for her life's work.

letters, contacted old friends, and ran hard. Her two opponents were experienced male politicians, each with strong support from part of the Republican party. She received barely 500 votes compared with her major opponent's total of more than 6,500. It was time to retire.

Ida B. Wells-Barnett continued to write her autobiography, which she had begun in the later 1920s. Wells-Barnett knew what a difference she had made in the lives of millions of Americans who had benefited from her work. She wanted future generations to know her story from her own point of view. (The book, edited by her granddaughter, was not to be published until almost 40 years after her death.) Ida B. Wells-Barnett was seldom one to give in to her own health problems. But after a day of shopping in Chicago on March 21, 1931, she returned home unusually tired. She didn't leave her bed for the rest of the day, still not complaining about being ill. The following morning, she was obviously very sick. Her loving family rushed her to a Chicago hospital. She was beyond help and died three days later, on the birthday of her first son, March 25, 1931, at the age of 69.

Ida B. Wells-Barnett's aggressiveness in stamping out injustice certainly offended some people, both white and black. Born into slavery and then thrown into adult responsibilities as a teenager, this beautiful, educated, and determined woman single-handedly raised a voice heard worldwide against lynching. She did not live to see a federal antilynching law passed. But she had done more than anyone else to publicize the problem and to help stop it. Ida B. Wells-Barnett worked to achieve a United States in which, as she wrote, "the liberty of each shall be the concern of all." As an educator, journalist, women's club movement leader, settlement house worker, probation officer, suffragist, and civil rights leader, she accomplished much that changed the way Americans live. All Americans are better off thanks to the gifts she gave us.

KEY DATES

July 6, 1862	Ida B. Wells is born in Holly Springs, Mississippi.
1863	Emancipation Proclamation goes into effect.
1865	The Civil War ends; the 13th Amendment ends slavery in all of the United States.
1868	The 14th Amendment makes former slaves full citizens and protects citizens from states trying to deny them their life, liberty, or property without due process of law; states are forbidden to deny citizens equal protection of the law.
1870	Mississippi rejoins the Union. The 15th Amendment declares that neither the U.S. government nor any state government can keep its citizens from voting because of their race, their color, or their having once been slaves.
1877	Union troops withdraw from occupation of the South, and Reconstruction ends.
1878	Yellow fever epidemic strikes Memphis, Tennessee, and surrounding region; James and Elizabeth Wells and their infant son, Stanley, die; Wells begins teaching to support her brothers and sisters.
1883	Wells moves to Memphis; Civil Rights Act of 1875 is declared unconstitutional.
1884	Wells is forced from first-class seating on the Chesapeake, Ohio & Southwestern Railroad; she successfully sues the railroad.
1885	Wells's sisters Annie and Lily move with an aunt to California.
1886	Wells begins writing in the *Living Way*, a religious newspaper; Wells visits her sisters in California.

1887	Tennessee Supreme Court overrules Wells's earlier victory against the Chesapeake, Ohio & Southwestern Railroad.
1889	Wells becomes part owner and editor of the *Free Speech*.
1891	Wells is fired from her teaching position in Memphis.
1892	Wells's friends Thomas Moss, Calvin McDowell, and Henry Stewart are lynched; *Free Speech* offices are ransacked; Wells's article "Exiles" is published in the *New York Age*; Wells gives her first antilynching speech; her booklet *Southern Horrors* is published.
1893	A Paris, Texas, lynching gets international coverage; Wells makes her first antilynching lecture tour of Great Britain; *The Reason Why the Colored American is Not in the World's Columbian Exposition* is published and distributed at the Chicago World's Fair; the Ida B. Wells Club is founded in Chicago.
1894	Wells again carries her antilynching campaign to Great Britain.
1895	Wells's *A Red Record* is published; Ferdinand L. Barnett and Ida B. Wells marry in Chicago.
1896	The *Plessy v. Ferguson* decision upholds the concept of "separate but equal."
1898	Wells-Barnett is named financial secretary of the Afro-American Council; she meets with President McKinley to urge that he push for a federal antilynching law; Wells-Barnett delivers a speech criticizing Booker T. Washington.
1900	Wells-Barnett's pamphlet *Mob Rule in New Orleans* is published.

1904	Wells-Barnett's essay "Booker T. Washington and His Critics" is published.
1905	Wells-Barnett helps found Niagara Movement.
1909	Wells-Barnett speaks out against lynching at the National Negro Conference; she investigates the Cairo, Illinois, lynching.
1909-1910	Wells-Barnett participates in the founding meetings of the NAACP.
1910	Wells-Barnett founds the Negro Fellowship League and the Light House.
1913	Wells-Barnett becomes an adult probation officer in Chicago; she helps organize the Alfa Suffrage Club.
1917	Wells-Barnett investigates the East St. Louis riots.
1919	Race riots occur in two dozen cities, including Chicago.
1920	The Light House closes; by means of the 19th Amendment, women gained the right to vote in national elections.
1922	Wells-Barnett investigates the Elaine, Arkansas, killings and writes *The Arkansas Race Riot*.
1930	Wells-Barnett runs for the Illinois State Senate.
1931	Wells-Barnett dies on March 25 in Chicago.

GLOSSARY

appeal To refer a court's decision to a higher court in an attempt to get the decision changed because of an error or injustice supposedly committed by the lower court.

apprentice One who is learning by practical experience a skill or craft from a skilled worker. The apprentice agrees to work for a set number of years for the skilled worker.

bigotry The acts or beliefs of a person who has an obstinate and unreasoning attachment to his or her own intolerant beliefs, opinions, and prejudices.

Black Codes A group of laws limiting the rights of African Americans adopted by some Southern states right after the Civil War.

boycott To join with others in refusing to purchase certain products or services or to have any dealings with a person, organization, or store. The purpose is to express disapproval or to force acceptance of certain demands.

discrimination Behavior that is unfair to a member or members of a particular racial, ethnic, religious, or other group, simply because they are members of that group, not because of their individual actions.

due process The legal process guaranteed under both the 5th and 14th Amendments to protect citizens from the government's stepping in and unlawfully taking away life, liberty, or property. Included in the due process concept are the basic rights of people accused in criminal trials and the established rules for fair trials.

epidemic The outbreak and rapid spread of a disease.

Jim Crow laws State and local laws passed in the South after the end of Reconstruction and designed to reduce the rights and freedoms of African Americans, often by legally enforcing discrimination and segregation.

lyceum An organization providing public lectures, concerts, and other entertainment, and generally furthering education.

missionary A person sent to spread religious beliefs and to convert others to a specific way of life, often accompanied by humanitarian activities.

poorhouse A place that used to be maintained at public expense to house needy or dependent people.

prejudice An opinion or belief not based on reasonable information, or formed before sufficient information is available. Prejudice is often an unreasoning attitude of hostility directed against an individual simply because he or she is a member of a particular religious, ethnic, racial, or other group.

probation officer An official appointed to investigate, report on, and supervise the conduct of convicted criminals who are not in prison but are under supervision as part of their sentence.

Reconstruction The reorganization and reestablishment of the seceded Southern states in the Union after the American Civil War. The Reconstruction period lasted until 1877.

segregation The unconstitutional policy and practice of separating or isolating members of a racial, ethnic, religious, or other group from other people. Segregation was enforced both by law and by tradition, resulting in discrimination and separation in housing, jobs, schools, and other places.

settlement house An organization providing various educational, recreational, medical, and other community services to people in poor, crowded city neighborhoods.

sharecropping Farming land for a landlord in return for a share of the crops. The sharecropper usually receives from the landlord, seeds, tools, supplies, living quarters, and credit for food and other items used before harvesting and is paid a specific share of the crop.

stereotype To make or have a standardized mental picture based on an oversimplified opinion, emotional attitude, or uncritical judgment, such as the opinion that all members of a group have the same qualities or act the same way.

strikebreaker A person hired to replace a striking worker. Striking workers sometimes call such a person a scab; employers may call a strikebreaker a replacement worker.

white supremacy The racist belief in the inborn superiority of whites over African Americans and therefore the belief in the need for and rightness of keeping Blacks, in an inferior political, social, and economic position in society.

BIBLIOGRAPHHY
and Recommended Reading

American Social History Project. *Who Built America? Working People and the Nation's Economy, Politics, Culture, and Society*. Vol. 2: *From the Gilded Age to the Present*. New York: Pantheon, 1992

Franklin, John Hope, and August Meier, eds. *Black Leaders of the Twentieth Century*. Urbana, Ill.: University of Illinois Press, 1982.

Hughes, Langston. *Fight for Freedom: The Story of the NAACP.* New York: W. W. Norton, 1962.

Loewenberg, Bert James, and Ruth Bogin, eds. *Black Women in Nineteenth Century American Life: Their Words, Their Thoughts, Their Feelings*. University Park, Pa.: The Pennsylvania State University Press, 1976.

*McCullough, David. *Ida B. Wells: A Passion for Justice*, PBS video (58 minutes), WGBH-TV: Boston. Alexandria, Va., 1983.

Shapiro, Herbert. *White Violence and Black Response: From Reconstruction to Montgomery*. Amherst, Mass.: University of Massachusetts Press, 1988.

Sterling, Dorothy, ed. *We Are Your Sisters: Black Women in the 19th Century*. New York: W. W. Norton, 1984.

Thompson, Mildred I. *Ida B. Wells-Barnett: An Exploratory Study of an American Black Woman, 1893-1930*. Brooklyn, N.Y.: Carlson Publishers, 1990.

*Van Steenwyck, Elizabeth. *Ida B. Wells-Barnett: Woman of Courage*. New York: Franklin Watts, 1992.

Wells, Ida B. *Crusade for Justice: The Autobiography of Ida B. Wells*. Edited by Alfreda M. Duster. Chicago, Ill.: University of Chicago Press, 1970.

Wells-Barnett, Ida B. *On Lynchings: Southern Horrors, A Red*

Record, Mob Rule in New Orleans. New York: Arno Press and The New York Times, 1969.

Zangrando, Robert L. *The NAACP Crusade Against Lynching, 1909-1950.* Philadelphia, Pa.: Temple University Press, 1980.

*Especially recommended for younger readers.

PLACES TO VISIT

Holly Springs, Mississippi
- Rust College, which Ida B. Wells attended when its name was Shaw University. Its library has a collection of materials about her.

- U.S. Postal Service's post office is named after Ida B. Wells. In 1990, the federal government issued an Ida B. Wells postage stamp to honor her.

INDEX

Aberdeen, 63
accommodationists, 74, 77, 83, 88–90, 92, 95
Addams, Jane, 84–85, 91
African Methodist Episcopal (AME) Church, 30–31, 32, 35, 37, 52, 53
Afro-American Council, 82, 83, 85–86, 91, 114
Alabama, 70, 72
Alcott, Louisa May, 30
Allen, Richard, 31
Alpha Suffrage Club, 102, 115
American Missionary Association, 33, 89
antilynching laws
  proposed federal, 81, 82, 95, 112, 114
  state, 68, 91
Anti-Lynching Society, 77
Arkansas, 109–110, 115
Arkansas Race Riot, The, 110, 115
Atlanta, 92
Atlanta University, 89
Atlantic Ocean, 62, 63

Barnett, Albert, 69
Barnett, Alfreda M., 80
Barnett, Charles Aked, 77, 79
Barnett, Ferdinand, Jr., 69
Barnett, Ferdinand L., 59, 65, 69–70, 71, 80, 81, 96–97, 98, 111, 114
Barnett, Herman K., 80, 81
Barnett, Ida B., 80
Barrett, W. H., 45
Beal Street Baptist Church, 38
Bible, 12, 16, 30, 98
Black Codes, 14, 17, 26, 27
Blair, Henry, 68
Bolling, Mr., 9, 10, 15
"Booker T. Washington and His Critics," 89–90, 114–115

Boston, 60, 62, 67, 77
boycotts, 50, 53
Brooklyn, 58–59
Brown, A. H., Mrs., 68
Brown, Henry B., 75
Bruce, Blanche K., 17
Butler, Fannie, 24, 34, 113

Cairo, 95–97, 100–101
California, 24, 33, 34, 36, 71, 113
Canada, 70, 91
Charles, Robert, 86–87
Chesapeake, Ohio, & Southwestern Railroad, 24, 26, 27–29, 30, 35, 36, 42, 44, 74, 113, 114
Chicago, 64, 65, 67, 68, 69, 70, 71, 79, 81, 83–84, 85, 88, 90, 92, 97–98, 99, 101, 102–103, 105, 106–108, 110, 114
Chicago Defender, 106, 110
Chicago Inter-Ocean, 67
Chicago Tribune, 47, 107
Chicago Urban League, 103
Chicago World's Fair. *See* World's Columbian Exposition
civil rights, 72, 74, 77, 82, 91, 98–99. *See also* voting and voting rights; 13th, 14th, 15th, 19th Amendments
Civil Rights Act of 1875, 26, 27, 36, 113
Civil Rights Cases decision of 1883, 26–27, 36
Civil War, 11, 12, 14, 17, 21, 47
Committee of Forty, 95, 97
Confederacy. *See* Confederate States of America
Confederate Army, 11
Confederate States of America, 11, 12
Conservator, 65, 69, 72, 80
cotton, 11, 12, 35, 53, 109
Countee, R. N., 31
County League of Clubs, 80

121

Coy, Ed, 62
Crisis, 97
Cuba, 82

Daily Commercial, 52
Daily News, 98
Dallas, 60
Davis, Frank, 96, 97, 100
Deneen, Charles S., 91, 96, 97, 100
Detroit Plaindealer, 33
Dickens, Charles, 30
discrimination, 14-15, 16, 17, 22, 26–27, 28, 29, 31–32, 33, 36, 38–39, 41, 45, 64, 65, 72, 74–76, 77, 86, 87, 91, 95, 97, 99–100, 102–103
Douglass, Frederick, 56, 57–58, 59, 62, 65, 72, 76, 79, 82
Douglass, Helen Pitts, 57, 79
Du Bois, W. E. B., 86, 88–89, 91–92, 93, 95, 97
due process of law, 14, 113
Duster, Alfreda M., 112

East St. Louis, 104–106, 108, 115
Elaine, 109–110, 115
Elevator, The, 34
Emancipation Proclamation, 11, 12, 93, 113
England, 56, 62, 63, 88
equal protection of the laws, 14, 26, 36–37, 50, 113
Evening Scimitar, 52–53
Evening Star, 33
"Exiled," 55, 56, 57, 114

Fellowship Herald, 101
15th Amendment, 14, 32, 39, 99, 113
Fisk, Clinton Bowen, 33
Fisk University, 33, 80
Flemming, J. L., 53, 54
Fort Erie, 91
Fortune, T. Thomas, 53, 54, 82, 86
14th Amendment, 14, 26, 27, 113
Frederick Douglass Center, 91

Freedmen's Aid Society, 16, 89
Freedmen's Bureau, 16, 33
freed people, 14, 16, 17
Freemasons, 18, 22
Free Speech, 38, 42, 44, 49–50, 52–54, 114

Garrison, William Lloyd, 93
Georgia, 68, 70, 92
Gray, Dr., 20, 21, 22
Great Chicago Fire of 1871, 65
Great Britain, 63, 67, 68, 69, 71, 114

Holly Springs, 12, 16, 17, 18, 20, 21, 22, 113
Hampton Institute and Industrial School, 72
Harvard University, 86
Havana, 82
Hoover, Herbert, 111
"How Enfranchisement Stops Lynching," 99–100
Hull House, 85
human rights, 72

"Ida B. Wells Abroad," 67
Ida B. Wells Club, 67, 68, 70, 79–80, 83, 114
Illinois, 68, 79, 91, 92, 96, 102, 115
Illinois State Senate, 111–112, 115
Illinois Woman's Republican State Committee, 71
Impey, Catherine, 62, 63
India, 62, 63
Indian Territory, 50, 70

James, William ("Frog"), 96
Jackson, 35
Jim Crow laws, 27, 31–32, 35, 39, 74, 86, 99. *See also* segregation
Joliet, 98

Kansas, 34
Kentucky, 68

Index

Ku Klux Klan (KKK), 39, 41, 47

labor unions, 103-104
Lake City, 81
Lawson, Mr. and Mrs. Victor, 98, 101
liberal arts education, 72, 89–90, 92
Light House, 98, 99, 101-102, 108–109, 115
Lincoln, Abraham, 11, 93
Little Rock, 110
Little Rock Sun, 33
Liverpool, 63
Living Way, 31, 38
London, 88
Louisiana, 74–75, 86
lyceum, 30, 33, 35, 37
lynching, 35, 45–47, 49–50, 51–54, 55, 56, 57, 58, 59, 60, 62, 67, 68, 70–71, 77, 81, 82, 85, 86, 87, 91, 93, 95–96, 97, 98, 99, 100–101, 114, 115
"Lynching: Our National Crime," 93, 95
lynch law, 55, 59, 68
Lyons, Maritcha, 58

McDowell, Calvin, 38, 45–46, 47, 48, 114
McKinley, William, 81, 82, 83, 114
Maine, 82
Manly, Alex, 82
Mason, William, 81
Massachusetts, 86
Mathews, Victoria, 58
Mayo, Isabelle, 62, 63
Memphis, 18, 19–20, 24, 27, 28, 30–32, 34, 36, 37–38, 39, 41, 42, 44–46, 48–50, 52–54, 55, 56, 68, 69, 113, 114
Memphis Daily Appeal, 29
Methodist Church, 31
Methodist Episcopal Church, 16
missionaries, 16, 17, 31
Mississippi, 9, 10, 11, 12, 14, 15, 16, 17, 24, 35, 48, 53, 68, 109, 113

Mississippi River, 18, 48, 105
Missouri, 48
Mob Rule in New Orleans, 87, 114
Mob Violence Act of 1905, 91, 96–97
"Mob Violence and Anarchy," 85
Moody, Dwight Lyman, 32
Moss, Betty, 37–38, 44, 48
Moss, Maurine, 37–38, 44, 48
Moss, Thomas, 37–38, 44, 45–46, 47, 48, 49, 50, 54, 63, 114

Nashville, 33
Natchez, 48
National Association for the Advancement of Colored People (NAACP), 97, 110, 115
National Association of Colored Women, 79, 83–84, 85, 110
National Education Association (NEA), 34
National Federation of Afro-American Women, 77, 79
National League of Colored Women, 79
National Negro Conference, 93, 95, 115
National Urban League, 103
National Woman's Christian Temperance Union, 67
Native Americans, 50
Negro Fellowship League, 98, 101, 103, 105, 106, 115
Negro Problem from the Negro Point of View, The, 89
New Hampshire, 68
New Orleans, 86–87
New York Age, 53, 54, 55, 56, 59, 114
New York City, 55, 58–59, 67
New York State, 70, 82, 91
New York State Cleveland League, 58
New York Times, 58, 59
Niagara Falls, 91
Niagara Movement, 91–92, 93, 95, 115
Nightingale, Taylor, 38, 42

19th Amendment, 108–109
North Carolina, 68, 82–83
Northwestern University, 70

Ohio, 68
Oklahoma, 50
Oklahoma Territory, 50, 52
Ontario, 91
Original Rights Magazine, 99

Pan-African Conference, 88
Paris, 60, 114
Peggy (Ida B. Wells's grandmother), 9, 15–16, 20, 24
Pennsylvania, 30
People's Grocery Company, 44, 45–46, 48, 49
Philadelphia, 30, 52, 53, 60, 62
Phillips County, 109
Plessy, Homer, 75
Plessy v. *Ferguson* decision, 75–76, 86, 114
public schools, 22, 23–24, 26, 27, 30, 33, 34, 36, 37, 41–42, 65, 76, 79, 90, 91, 100
Pulaski, 39

race riots, 82, 83, 86–87, 88, 92–93, 95–98, 100, 104–106, 107–108, 109, 115
Reason Why the Colored American is Not in the World's Columbian Exposition, The, 65, 114
Reconstruction period, 12, 14, 17, 21, 22–23, 26, 36, 39, 113
Red Record, A, 70–71, 114
religion, 12, 16, 17, 27, 30–31, 32, 35, 37, 38, 65, 69, 71, 90, 93, 98
Republican party, 71, 79, 83, 111–112
Revolutionary War, 47
Richmond, 12
Rochester, 82
Rust College. *See* Shaw University

St. Louis, 48, 105
Salzner, Henry, 96
San Francisco, 34
Sankey, Ira David, 32
Scotland, 62, 63
segregation, 27, 28, 29, 31–32, 33, 34–35, 36–37, 41–42, 45, 62, 63, 67, 69, 72, 74–75, 86, 88, 90–91, 92, 95, 97, 99–100, 103
Shakespeare, William, 30
sharecropping and sharecroppers, 17, 22, 23, 109
Shaw University, 16, 17, 30
Shelby County, 24, 27
slavery, 9, 10–11, 12, 14, 15, 17, 21, 32, 47, 69, 70, 72, 79, 93, 113
Society for the Recognition of the Brotherhood of Man, 63
Souls of Black Folk, The, 88
South Carolina, 68, 81
Southern Horrors: Lynch Law in Its Phases, 59, 114
Springfield, 92, 96, 100, 106
Stewart, Henry, 38, 45–46, 47, 48, 114

Tennessee, 18, 24, 27, 28, 36, 37, 39, 44, 68, 69, 109, 113, 114
Tennessee Supreme Court, 36, 37, 44, 114
Terrell, Mary Church, 84
terrorism, 39, 41, 47, 52–53, 68, 88, 92. *See also* lynching
Texas, 60, 68, 114
13th Amendment, 13–14
Tippah County, 9, 13, 20
Topeka, 34
Tubman, Harriet, 79
Tuskegee Normal and Industrial Institute, 72, 90

U.S. Army, 11, 17
U.S. Congress, 11, 16, 26
U.S. Constitution, 12, 14, 26, 31, 32, 75, 77, 79, 99, 108

Index

U.S. House of Representatives, 68
U.S. Supreme Court, 26–27, 74, 75–76, 86

Villard, Oswald Garrison, 93, 97
Virginia, 9, 72
Visalia, 24, 34
vocational education, 72, 89, 92
voting and voting rights, 14, 15, 17, 26, 32, 39, 48, 67, 70, 71, 72, 77, 79, 82, 83, 92, 97, 99–100, 102, 108–109, 112, 113, 115

Washington, Booker T., 72, 74, 76, 77, 84, 85–86, 88, 89–90, 92, 93, 95, 114
Washington, Margaret Murray, 77, 79
Washington, D.C., 60, 79, 102
Wells, Annie, 17, 21–22, 24, 33, 34, 71, 113
Wells, Eddie, 16
Wells, Elizabeth Warrenton ("Lizzie"), 9–10, 11, 12, 15, 16, 20, 70, 113
Wells, Eugenia ("Genie"), 16, 21, 22, 24, 33
Wells, George, 16, 21, 22, 24, 33
Wells, Ida B. (Ida B. Wells-Barnett)
  active in Republican party, 71, 79, 81, 111–112
  adult probation officer, 100–101, 112
  antilynching campaign, 47, 48, 49–54, 55, 56–60, 62–64, 67, 68, 70–71, 77, 81–82, 83, 85, 86, 87, 93–95, 96–97, 98, 114–115
  attends National Negro Conference, 93–95, 115
  becomes a full-time journalist, 44
  becomes part owner and editor of the *Free Speech*, 38, 114
  birth of, 9, 11, 113
  birth of her children, 77, 80
  care of her sisters and brothers, 22–24, 34, 113
  character and personality, 20, 22, 28, 30, 31, 32, 33, 37, 41, 42, 49, 53–54, 57, 59, 68–69, 80, 84, 85, 90, 91, 97, 98, 102, 110, 112
  childhood of, 11, 12, 16–17
  church activities of, 30–31, 32, 35, 37, 38, 42, 52, 65, 98
  conflicts with other African Americans, 34–35, 41, 42, 53, 57, 58, 63, 65, 71, 77, 79, 83, 84, 89–90, 91, 92, 97, 103, 106, 114
  death of, 112, 115
  death of her parents, 9, 20, 34, 70, 113
  destruction of the *Free Speech* offices, 53
  early years as a slave, 11, 12
  editor of *Fellowship Herald*, 101
  education of, 12, 16, 17, 22, 30, 33, 35, 37
  establishes the Light House, 98
  fame of, 50, 53, 98, 112
  founding of Ida B. Wells Club, 67
  friendship with Frederick and Helen Douglass, 57–58, 79
  helps found Afro-American Council, 82, 114
  helps found Alpha Suffrage Club, 102, 115
  helps found NAACP, 97, 115
  helps found the Niagara Movement, 91–92, 115
  helps found the Society for the Recognition of the Brotherhood of Man, 63
  helps organize Illinois Woman's Republican State Committee, 71
  impact on her of lynching of Thomas Moss, 47, 49–50, 114
  investigates race riots, 106–107, 110
  lawsuit against the Chesapeake, Ohio, & Southwestern Railroad, 28–29, 30, 35, 36, 42, 44, 74, 113
  lectures and lecture tours of, 58,

59, 60, 62, 63, 65, 67, 68, 70, 79, 83, 93, 95, 110, 114
life in Memphis, 29, 30–34, 35, 36, 37–39, 41–42, 44–47, 48–50, 52–54
marriage of, 70, 71, 114
moves to Chicago, 65
moves to New York City, 55
opposes discrimination and segregation, 28–29, 30, 34–35, 36, 41–42, 77
organizes Negro Fellowship League, 98
pen name of "Iola," 31, 36, 58
presents antilynching proposal to President McKinley, 81, 114
purchases the *Conservator,* 72
runs for Illinois State Senate, 111–112, 115
serves on Committee of Forty, 95
takes name Ida B. Wells-Barnett, 72
teacher, 22, 23–24, 27, 30, 33, 34, 36, 37, 41–42, 44, 79, 113, 114
works for women's rights, 41, 44, 71, 79, 83
writing, 31, 32, 33, 34–35, 36, 37, 38–39, 41–42, 44, 49, 50, 52, 53–54, 55, 56, 59, 60, 65, 67, 69, 72, 87, 93, 99–101, 106, 107–108, 110, 112, 114
See also: Arkansas Race Riot, The; "Booker T. Washington and His Critics"; "Exiled"; "How Enfranchisement Stops Lynching"; "Ida B. Wells Abroad"; "Lynching: Our National Crime"; *Mob Rule in New Orleans;* "Mob Violence and Anarchy"; *Reason Why the Colored American is Not in the World's Columbian Exposition, The; Red Record, A*

Wells, James (father), 9, 10, 11, 14–15, 16–17, 20, 21, 55, 70, 113
Wells, James (brother), 16, 21, 22, 24, 33
Wells, Lily, 17, 21, 22, 24, 33, 34, 71, 113
Wells, Stanley, 17, 21, 34, 113
white supremacy, 41, 52, 82–83
Willard, Frances, 67
Williams, S. Laing, 59
Wilmington, 82, 83
Wilmington Record, 82, 83
Wilson, Woodrow, 102
women's clubs, 59–60, 65, 67, 71, 77, 79, 81, 83–84, 91, 102, 115
Women's Loyal Union, 59
women's rights, 41, 44, 59, 67, 72, 77, 79, 81, 85, 99, 108, 115
Wooley, Celia Parker, 91
World's Columbian Exposition, 63, 64, 65, 67, 114
World's Woman's Christian Temperance Union, 67
World War I, 102, 103–104, 106

yellow fever epidemic, 9, 18–20, 21, 24, 70, 113
YMCA, 98, 101

Richard M. Haynes is the Director of Field Experiences and Teacher Placement and Assistant Professor in the Department of Administration, Curriculum, and Instruction in the School of Education and Psychology at Western Carolina University in Cullowhee, North Carolina. This is his seventh book. Dr. Haynes writes primarily history books, often centering around Southern history for young adults. He and his wife, Dianne, and their daughters, Lisa and Heather, live in Waynesville, North Carolina.

James P. Shenton is Professor of History at Columbia University. He has taught American History since 1951. Among his publications are *Robert John Walker, a Politician from Jackson to Lincoln; An Historian's History of the United States*; and *The Melting Pot*. Professor Shenton is a consultant to the National Endowment for the Humanities and has received the Mark Van Doren and Society of Columbia Graduates' Great Teachers Awards. He also serves as a consultant for CBS, NBC, and ABC educational programs.

COVER ILLUSTRATION
Gary McElhaney

MAPS
Go Media, Inc.

PHOTOGRAPHY CREDITS
p.6 Department of Special Collections, University of Chicago Library; p.10 New York Historical Society; p.13 Library of Congress; pp. 15, 19, 23, 40, 46 The Bettmann Archive; p.51 Department of Special Collections, University of Chicago Library; p.61 The Bettmann Archive; p.63 The Granger Collection; p.66 UPI/Bettmann; p.73 The Library of Congress; p.75 Historical New Orleans Collection; p.78 Department of Special Collections, University of Chicago Library; pp.80, 84 The Library of Congress; p.85 University of Illinois Library at Chicago Circle Campus Jane Addams Memorial Collection; p.88 The Library of Congress; p.94 Department of Special Collections, University of Chicago Library; p.104 UPI/Bettmann; p.105 The Granger Collection; p.107 Department of Special Collections, University of Chicago Library; p.108 The Library of Congress; p.109 The Granger Collection; p.111 Department of Special Collections, University of Chicago Library.

ACKNOWLEDGMENTS

The author acknowledges with gratitude permission from publishers to quote from their works:

Duster, Alfreda M., ed., *Crusade for Justice: The Autobiography of Ida B. Wells*, Chicago: University of Chicago Press, 1970; Katz, William Loren, ed., *On Lynchings: Southern Horrors, A Red Record, Mob Rule in New Orleans*, Salem, N.H.: Ayer Company Publishers, 1969; Lefler, Hugh Talmage, and Albert Newsome, *The History of a Southern State: North Carolina*, 3rd ed., Chapel Hill: The University of North Carolina Press, 1973; Loewenberg, Bert James, and Ruth Bogin, eds., *Black Women in Nineteenth Century American Life: Their Words, Their Thoughts, Their Feelings*, University Park, Pa.: The Pennsylvania State University Press, 1976; Sterling, Dorothy, ed., *We Are Your Sisters: Black Women in the 19th Century*, New York: W. W. Norton, 1984; Thompson, Mildred I., *Ida B. Wells-Barnett: An Exploratory Study of an American Black Woman, 1893–1930*, Brooklyn, N.Y.: Carlson Publishing Inc., 1990; Zangrando, Robert L., *The NAACP Crusade Against Lynching, 1909–1930*, Philadelphia: Temple University Press, 1980. All reasonable efforts were made to contact the copyright holders.